LANGUAGE for WRITING

Siegfried Engelmann • Jean Osborn

TEXTBOOK

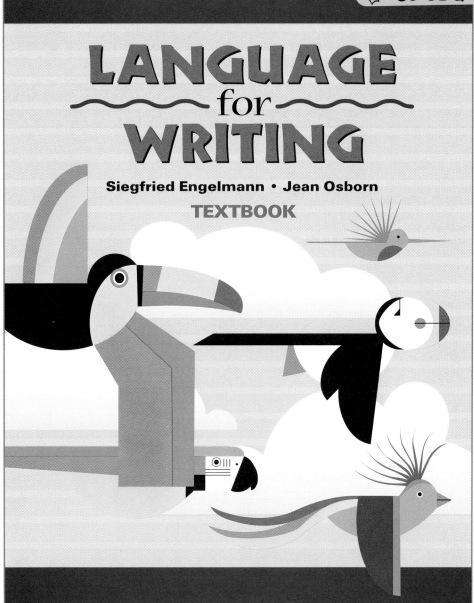

Columbus, Ohio

The **McGraw·Hill** Companies

SRAonline.com

 **SRA**

Send all inquiries to:
SRA/McGraw-Hill
8787 Orion Place
Columbus, OH 43240-4027

0-07-600356-6

5 6 7 8 9 QWT 09 08 07 06

TABLE OF CONTENTS

Lesson 1	1		Lesson 38	51
Lesson 2	2		Lesson 39	53
Lesson 3	3		Lesson 40	55
Lesson 4	4		Lesson 41	57
Lesson 5	5		Lesson 42	59
Lesson 6	6		Lesson 43	62
Lesson 7	7		Lesson 44	65
Lesson 8	8		Lesson 45	68
Lesson 9	9		Lesson 46	70
Lesson 10	10		Lesson 47	73
Lesson 11	11		Lesson 48	76
Lesson 12	12		Lesson 49	79
Lesson 13	13		Lesson 50	82
Lesson 14	14		Lesson 51	85
Lesson 15	15		Lesson 52	87
Lesson 16	16		Lesson 53	89
Lesson 17	17		Lesson 54	91
Lesson 18	18		Lesson 55	94
Lesson 19	19		Lesson 56	97
Lesson 20	20		Lesson 57	99
Lesson 21	21		Lesson 58	102
Lesson 22	23		Lesson 59	104
Lesson 23	25		Lesson 60	107
Lesson 24	27		Lesson 61	110
Lesson 25	29		Lesson 62	113
Lesson 26	31		Lesson 63	115
Lesson 27	32		Lesson 64	117
Lesson 28	34		Lesson 65	119
Lesson 29	35		Lesson 66	121
Lesson 30	36		Lesson 67	123
Lesson 31	37		Lesson 68	125
Lesson 32	39		Lesson 69	127
Lesson 33	41		Lesson 70	129
Lesson 34	43		Lesson 71	131
Lesson 35	45		Lesson 72	133
Lesson 36	47		Lesson 73	136
Lesson 37	49		Lesson 74	139

TABLE OF CONTENTS

Continued

Lesson 75 . . . . **142**	Lesson 108 . . . . **217**
Lesson 76 . . . . **144**	Lesson 109 . . . . **220**
Lesson 77 . . . . **147**	Lesson 110 . . . . **222**
Lesson 78 . . . . **149**	Lesson 111 . . . . **224**
Lesson 79 . . . . **152**	Lesson 112 . . . . **226**
Lesson 80 . . . . **155**	Lesson 113 . . . . **228**
Lesson 81 . . . . **157**	Lesson 114 . . . . **229**
Lesson 82 . . . . **160**	Lesson 115 . . . . **230**
Lesson 83 . . . . **163**	Lesson 116 . . . . **231**
Lesson 84 . . . . **165**	Lesson 117 . . . . **232**
Lesson 85 . . . . **168**	Lesson 118 . . . . **234**
Lesson 86 . . . . **171**	Lesson 119 . . . . **235**
Lesson 87 . . . . **173**	Lesson 120 . . . . **237**
Lesson 88 . . . . **175**	Lesson 121 . . . . **238**
Lesson 89 . . . . **177**	Lesson 122 . . . . **239**
Lesson 90 . . . . **179**	Lesson 123 . . . . **241**
Lesson 91 . . . . **181**	Lesson 124 . . . . **242**
Lesson 92 . . . . **183**	Lesson 125 . . . . **243**
Lesson 93 . . . . **185**	Lesson 126 . . . . **244**
Lesson 94 . . . . **187**	Lesson 127 . . . . **245**
Lesson 95 . . . . **189**	Lesson 128 . . . . **246**
Lesson 96 . . . . **191**	Lesson 129 . . . . **247**
Lesson 97 . . . . **193**	Lesson 130 . . . . **248**
Lesson 98 . . . . **195**	Lesson 131 . . . . **249**
Lesson 99 . . . . **197**	Lesson 132 . . . . **251**
Lesson 100 . . . . **200**	Lesson 133 . . . . **253**
Lesson 101 . . . . **203**	Lesson 134 . . . . **254**
Lesson 102 . . . . **205**	Lesson 135 . . . . **255**
Lesson 103 . . . . **207**	Lesson 136 . . . . **257**
Lesson 104 . . . . **209**	Lesson 137 . . . . **260**
Lesson 105 . . . . **211**	Lesson 138 . . . . **262**
Lesson 106 . . . . **213**	Lesson 139 . . . . **264**
Lesson 107 . . . . **215**	Lesson 140 . . . . **266**

Use a sheet of lined paper for your work.

Write two sentences about the picture.

dog	table	sitting	window
sad	afraid	feels	floor

STOP END OF LESSON 1.

1

# LESSON 2

Use a sheet of lined paper for your work.

Write two sentences about the picture.

elephant	tree	shade	feels

 END OF LESSON 2.

2

Write two sentences about the picture.

| boy | head | dizzy | standing | upside down | feels |

 END OF LESSON 3.

LESSON 4

A. Follow the directions for each item.

1. Draw a horizontal line on your paper.
2. Draw a vertical line on your paper.
3. Make a dot on your paper.

B. Write two sentences about the picture.

monkey	banana	wants	one	eating	other	feels

 END OF LESSON 4.

4

A. Follow the directions for each item.

1. Draw a rectangle on your paper.
2. Draw a triangle on your paper.
3. Draw a circle on your paper.

B. Write two sentences about the picture. In the first sentence tell what the boy is doing. In the second sentence tell how the boy feels.

boat	sitting	happy	smiling	feels

STOP END OF LESSON 5.

A. Follow the directions for each item.

1. Draw a triangle on your paper.
2. Draw a rectangle on your paper.
3. Draw a circle on your paper.

B. Write two sentences about the picture. In the first sentence tell what the girl is doing. In the second sentence tell how the girl feels.

floor	chair	waving	broken	angry

 END OF LESSON 6.

6

A. Write the answers to the questions on your paper.

Stoon is a silly word for table.

1. What is a stoon?
2. What parts does a stoon have?
3. Name a class that a stoon is in.

B. Follow the directions for each item.

1. First draw a horizontal line on your paper.
2. Then draw a rectangle above the horizontal line.
3. Then make a dot inside the rectangle.

C. Write two sentences about the picture. In the first sentence tell what the man is doing. In the second sentence tell how the man feels.

| bucket | sponge | washing | proud | feels |

 END OF LESSON 7.

7

A. Write the answers to the questions on your paper.

Niz is a silly word for chair.

1. What is a niz?
2. Name a class that a niz is in.
3. What parts does a niz have?
4. What do you do with a niz?

B. Follow the directions.

1. First draw a rectangle on your paper.
2. Then draw a circle inside the rectangle.
3. Then make a dot inside the circle.

C. Write two sentences about the picture. In the first sentence tell what the girl is doing. In the second sentence tell how the girl feels.

slide	happy	dizzy	feels

STOP END OF LESSON 8.

8

A. Write the answers to the questions on your paper.

Ging is a silly word for pencil.

1. What is a ging?
2. What parts does a ging have?
3. What do you do with a ging?
4. Name a class that a ging is in.

B. Write two sentences about the picture. In the first sentence tell what the girl is doing. In the second sentence tell how the girl feels.

| girl | patting | kind | happy | kneeling |

Independent Work

C. Follow the directions.

1. First draw a horizontal line on your paper.
2. Then make a dot above the horizontal line.
3. Then draw a triangle below the horizontal line.

 END OF LESSON 9.

9

A. Write the answers to the questions on your paper.

Fuf is a silly word for shovel.

1. What is a fuf?
2. Name a class that a fuf is in.
3. What part does a fuf have?
4. What do you do with a fuf?

B. Write two sentences about the picture. In the first sentence, tell what the boy is doing. In the second sentence, tell how the boy feels.

| boy | running | from | afraid | excited | squirrel |

Independent Work

C. Follow the directions.

1. First draw a circle on your paper.
2. Then draw a horizontal line above the circle.
3. Then draw a vertical line inside the circle.

 END OF LESSON 10.

A. Write two sentences about the picture.

ladder	standing	wall	painting	room

Independent Work

B. Follow the directions.

1. First draw a rectangle on your paper.
2. Then draw a circle inside the rectangle.
3. Then draw a triangle above the rectangle.

 END OF LESSON 11.

LESSON 12

A. Write two sentences about the picture.

| doghouse | bone | chewing |

Independent Work

B. Write the answers to the questions.

Nozo is a silly word for table.

1. What is a nozo?
2. What parts does a nozo have?
3. Name a class that a nozo is in.

 END OF LESSON 12.

12

A. Write two sentences about the picture.

| girl | hair | combing | swing |

Independent Work

B. Follow the directions.

1. First draw a vertical line on your paper.
2. Then draw a horizontal line below the vertical line.
3. Then make a dot below the horizontal line.

 **STOP** END OF LESSON 13.

A. Write two sentences about the picture.

playing	monkey	truck	piano

Independent Work

B. Write the answers to the questions.

Rup is a silly word for wagon.

1. What is a rup?
2. What parts does a rup have?
3. What material is a rup made of?

 END OF LESSON 14.

A. Write two sentences about the picture. Your first sentence will tell where the dog is. Your second sentence will tell what the dog is doing.

fish	lake	swimming	water

Independent Work

B. Follow the directions.

1. First make a dot on your paper.
2. Then draw a circle around the dot.
3. Then draw a horizontal line above the circle.

 END OF LESSON 15.

A. Write two sentences about the picture. Your first sentence will tell where the woman is. Your second sentence will tell what the woman is doing.

oven	cake	kitchen	woman

Independent Work

B. Write the answers to the questions.

Jow is a silly word for kite.

1. What is a jow?
2. Name a class that a jow is in.
3. What do you do with a jow?

STOP END OF LESSON 16.

16

A. Write two sentences.

1. Write a sentence that tells about **a funny girl.**
2. Write a sentence that tells about **five red birds.**

B. Write two sentences about the picture. Your first sentence will tell where the squirrel is. Your second sentence will tell what the squirrel is doing.

porch	nut	eating	squirrel

Independent Work

C. Follow the directions.

1. First draw a vertical line on your paper.
2. Then draw a triangle above the vertical line.
3. Then draw a rectangle below the vertical line.

 END OF LESSON 17.

A. Write two sentences.

1. Write a sentence that tells about **two old pigs.**
2. Write a sentence that tells about **my dog.**

B. Write two sentences about the picture. Your first sentence will tell where the girl is. Your second sentence will tell what the girl is doing.

| car | reading | book |

Independent Work

C. Write the answers to the questions.

Clup is a silly word for bookcase.

1. What is a clup?
2. Name a class that a clup is in.
3. What do you put in a clup?

 END OF LESSON 18.

18

A. Write two sentences about the picture. Your first sentence will tell where the man is. Your second sentence will tell what the man is doing.

| house | watching | roof | TV |

Independent Work

B. Write two sentences.

1. Write a sentence that tells about **that old bottle.**
2. Write a sentence that tells about **one elephant.**

C. Follow the directions.

1. First draw a circle on your paper.
2. Then draw a rectangle around the circle.
3. Then draw a horizontal line below the rectangle.

 **STOP** END OF LESSON 19.

A. Write two sentences about the picture. Your first sentence will tell where the cow is. Your second sentence will tell what the cow is doing.

| cow | pool | swimming |

Independent Work

B. Write two sentences.

1. Write a sentence that tells about **the black horse.**
2. Write a sentence that tells about **those books.**

C. Write the answers to the questions.

Lopo is a silly word for brush.

1. What is a lopo?
2. What parts does a lopo have?
3. What do you do with a lopo?

 END OF LESSON 20.

A. Write what each of the funny words means.

1. An **unger** is an eating tool.
   You use an **unger** to eat soup.

   An unger is a ____ .

2. A **muko** is a piece of clothing.
   You wear a **muko** on your foot.
   A **muko** has laces.

   A muko is a ____ .

B. Write two sentences.

1. Write a sentence that asks a question about **the bird.**
2. Write a sentence that asks a question about **the three big dogs.**

C. Write two sentences about the dogs. Tell where the dogs are. Then tell what the dogs are doing.

turtle	are	standing	howling

Independent Work

D. Follow the directions.

1. First draw a vertical line on your paper.
2. Then draw a circle around the vertical line.
3. Then draw a horizontal line above the circle.

STOP END OF LESSON 21.

A. Write two sentences.

1. Write a sentence that asks a question about **Mary's dress.**
2. Write a sentence that asks a question about **the man and the boy.**

B. Write what each of the funny words means.

1. A **vorg** is a large container.
   A **vorg** is often made of plastic.
   You put garbage in a **vorg.**

   A vorg is a _____ .

2. A **swib** is a large vehicle.
   It is made of metal.
   A **swib** has wings.

   A swib is an _____ .

C. Write two sentences about the boys. Tell where the boys are. Then tell what the boys are doing.

boys	playground	baseball
	throwing	catch

Independent Work

D. Write the answers to the questions.

Rappo is a silly word for table.

1. What is a rappo?
2. What parts does a rappo have?
3. What do you do with a rappo?
4. Name a class that a rappo is in.

 END OF LESSON 22.

24

A. Write two sentences.

   1. Write a sentence that asks a question about **these oranges.**

   2. Write a sentence that asks a question about **that big bird.**

B. Write what each of the funny words means.

   1. A **glurk** is found in the kitchen.
     It has a door and shelves.
     A **glurk** is used to keep food cold.

     A glurk is a   .

   2. A **snork** has a tail and four legs.
     It also has a trunk.

     A snork is an   .

C. Write two sentences about the cat. Tell where the cat is. Then tell what the cat is doing.

sled	sitting	horses

Independent Work

D. Follow the directions.

1. First draw a square on your paper.
2. Then draw a vertical line below the square.
3. Then draw a triangle inside the square.

STOP END OF LESSON 23.

A. Write what each funny word means.

1. A **taku** is made of metal.
   It is round with a hole in the middle.
   You wear a **taku** on your finger.

   A taku is a   .

2. A **noote** is a tall plant.
   It has a trunk, branches and leaves.
   Children like to climb a **noote.**

   A noote is a   .

B. Write two sentences about the lions. Tell where the lions are. Then tell what the lions are doing.

sleeping	lions	zoo

Independent Work

C. Write two sentences.

1. Write a sentence that asks a question about **my pet frog.**
2. Write a sentence that tells about **my pet frog.**

D. Write the answers to the questions.

Vig is a silly word for jar.

1. What is a vig?
2. Name a class that a vig is in.
3. What do you do with a vig?

STOP END OF LESSON 24.

A. Write two sentences about the picture. Tell where the fish tank is.
Then tell what the fish are doing.

bathtub	fish tank	bathroom	jumping

Independent Work

B. Follow the directions.

   1. First draw a triangle on your paper.
   2. Then make a dot inside the triangle.
   3. Then draw a circle around the triangle.
   4. Then draw a square around the circle.

C. Write sentences.

   1. Write a sentence that asks a question about **my wagon.**
   2. Write a sentence that asks a question about **those seven elephants.**

D. Write what each of the funny words means.

   1. A **mimak** is made of wood.
      It has a point and an eraser.
      You write with a **mimak.**

      A mimak is a   .

   2. A **blerk** is an animal with four legs.
      It lives on the farm.
      A **blerk** is very fat and loves to play in the mud.

      A blerk is a   .

STOP END OF LESSON 25.

A. Write two sentences about the girls. Tell where the girls are. Then tell what the girls are doing.

basketball court	playing

Independent Work

B. Write the answers to the questions.

Gofu is a silly word for book.

1. What is a gofu?
2. What parts does a gofu have?
3. What do you do with a gofu?

C. Write two sentences.

1. Write a sentence that tells about **the tall girls.**
2. Write a sentence that asks a question about **a tiger.**

 **STOP** END OF LESSON 26.

A. Write two sentences about the men. Tell where the men are. Then tell what the men are doing.

roof	fixing	men

Independent Work

B. Write two sentences.

1. Write a sentence that asks a question about **the apple trees.**
2. Write a sentence that tells about **the apple trees.**

C. Follow the directions.

1. First draw a square on your paper.
2. Then draw a circle inside the square.
3. Then make a dot inside the circle.
4. Then draw a triangle above the square.

D. Write what the funny word means.

A **ferb** has a handle and a blade with teeth.
It is used to cut wood.

A ferb is a .

STOP END OF LESSON 27.

A. Write two sentences about the monkeys. Tell where the monkeys are. Then tell what the monkeys are doing.

books	monkeys	reading

Independent Work

B. Write sentences.

1. Write a sentence that tells about **a big truck.**
2. Write a sentence that tells about **the frog and the turtle.**

C. Write the answers to the questions.

Zor is a silly word for wagon.

1. What is a zor?
2. Name a class that a zor is in.
3. What parts does a zor have?

 END OF LESSON 28.

34

A. Write two sentences about the dogs. Tell where the dogs are. Then tell what the dogs are doing.

map	looking

Independent Work

B. Write sentences.

1. Write a sentence that asks a question about **that blue bottle.**
2. Write a sentence that tells about **that blue bottle.**

C. Follow the directions.

1. First draw a rectangle on your paper.
2. Then draw a square above the rectangle.
3. Then draw a triangle below the rectangle.
4. Then draw a vertical line next to the rectangle.

 END OF LESSON 29.

A. Write two sentences about the cows. Tell where the cows are. Then tell what the cows are doing.

field	farmer	chasing

Independent Work

B. Write the answers to the questions.

Wapa is a silly word for glove.

1. What is a wapa?
2. What materials is a wapa made of?
3. What do you do with a wapa?
4. Name a class that a wapa is in.

C. Write sentences.

1. Write a sentence that asks a question about **that monkey.**
2. Write a sentence that tells about **her yellow hat.**

STOP END OF LESSON 30.

A. Write sentences about this picture.

1. Write two or more sentences about what you see in the picture.
2. Write one sentence about how the boy feels.

blowing	birthday	candles
party	presents	balloons

Independent Work

B. Write the answers to the questions.

Tupo is a silly word for nail.

1. What is a tupo?
2. What material is a tupo made of?
3. Where do you see a tupo?

C. Follow the directions.

1. First draw a rectangle on your paper.
2. Then draw a circle above the rectangle.
3. Then draw a horizontal line below the rectangle.
4. Then draw a horizontal line above the circle.

D. Write synonyms and opposites.

1. Write a synonym for each word.
   a. above   b. shut   c. easy

2. Write the opposite of each word.
   a. short   b. asleep   c. different

E. Write two sentences.

1. Write a sentence that tells about **a baby rabbit.**
2. Write a sentence that tells about **two turtles.**

STOP END OF LESSON 31.

A. Write sentences about this picture.

1. Write two or more sentences about what you see in the picture.
2. Write one sentence about how the woman feels.

| raining | hole | woman | umbrella |

Independent Work

B. Write two sentences.

1. Write a sentence that tells about **five kittens.**
2. Write a sentence that tells about **the green tent.**

C. Write synonyms and opposites.

1. Write a synonym for each word.
   a. quick   b. difficult   c. alike

2. Write the opposite for each word.
   a. win   b. easy   c. open

D. Follow the directions.

1. First draw a triangle on your paper.
2. Then draw a circle inside the triangle.
3. Then draw a rectangle around the triangle.
4. Then make a dot inside the circle.

E. Write what each of the funny words means.

1. A **migli** is an eating tool. It has a handle and a blade.

   A migli is a   .

2. A **hoxo** is part of the body. It has fingers, nails and a palm. You have two of them.

   A hoxo is a   .

STOP END OF LESSON 32.

40

A. Write sentences about this picture.

1. Write two or more sentences about what you see in the picture.
2. Write one sentence about how the girl feels.

balloons	bunch	afraid	barking

Independent Work

B. Follow the directions.

1. First draw a rectangle on your paper.
2. Then draw a horizontal line below the rectangle.
3. Then make a dot inside the rectangle.
4. Then draw a line from the dot to one end of the horizontal line.

C. Write two sentences.

1. Write a sentence that tells about **her new dress.**
2. Write a sentence that tells about **the ants.**

D. Write the answers to the questions.

Spoo is a silly word for hammer.

1. What is a spoo?
2. What do you do with a spoo?
3. What parts does a spoo have?
4. Name a class that a spoo is in.

STOP END OF LESSON 33.

A. Write each sentence, but leave out one of the words. Put a comma in place of that word.

1. That girl ran and slipped and fell down.
2. The girls drank milk and water and juice.
3. Carol will buy carrots or beans or corn.

B. Write sentences about this picture.

1. Write two or more sentences about what you see in the picture.
2. Write one sentence about how the dog feels.

wagging	bucket	tail	water
happy	thirsty	standing	carrying

Independent Work

C. Write two sentences.

1. Write a sentence that tells about **her new coat.**
2. Write a sentence that asks a question about **her new coat.**

D. Follow the directions.

1. First draw a triangle on your paper.
2. Then draw a circle next to the triangle.
3. Then draw a rectangle around both the triangle and the circle.
4. Then draw a horizontal line above the rectangle.

E. Write synonyms and opposites.

1. Write a synonym for each word.
   a. quick   b. shiny   c. same

2. Write the opposite of each word.
   a. wide   b. outside   c. up

STOP END OF LESSON 34.

A. Write each sentence, but leave out one of the words. Put a comma in place of that word.

1. The hungry man ate peas and beans and corn.
2. Sue washed the car and the bike and the wagon.
3. Tom and Bill and Hasaan went to school.

B. Write sentences about this picture.

1. Write two or more sentences about what you see in the picture.
2. Write one sentence about how the man feels.

hole	tree	plant	shovel	leaning

Independent Work

C. Write two sentences.

1. Write a sentence that asks a question about **his socks.**
2. Write a sentence that tells about **his socks.**

D. Write what each of the funny words means.

1. A **zordo** is found in a bedroom. It has blankets and sheets. You sleep in a zordo.

    A **zordo** is a ⬜ .

2. A **taga** is a piece of furniture with a back and a seat. It is big enough for only one person to sit on.

    A **taga** is a ⬜ .

E. Follow the directions.

1. First make two dots on your paper.
2. Then draw a circle around the two dots.
3. Then draw a horizontal line above the circle.
4. Then draw a horizontal line below the circle.

STOP END OF LESSON 35.

A. Write each sentence, but leave out one of the words. Put a comma in place of that word.

1. The boy put on his hat and coat and gloves.
2. The boys could ride bikes or skateboards or scooters.
3. Miguel wanted to visit his aunt and uncle and cousin.

B. Write sentences about this picture.

1. Write two or more sentences about what you see in the picture.
2. Write one sentence about how the boy feels.

fence	mud	puddle	afraid	dirty

Independent Work

C. Follow the directions.

1. First make a dot on your paper.
2. Then make another dot below the first dot.
3. Then draw a rectangle below the two dots.
4. Then draw a circle around the two dots and the rectangle.

D. Write synonyms and opposites.

1. Write a synonym for each word.
   a. shout   b. quiet   c. near

2. Write the opposite of each word.
   a. lose   b. easy   c. shut

E. Write the answers to the questions.

Yaso is a silly word for broom.

1. What is a yaso?
2. What parts does a yaso have?
3. What do you do with a yaso?
4. Name a class that a yaso is in.

STOP END OF LESSON 36.

A. Write sentences about this picture.

1. Write two or more sentences about what you see in the picture.
2. Write one sentence about how the boy feels.

| water | shivering | afraid | foot | lifeguard |

LIFEGUARD

Independent Work

B. Write each sentence, but leave out one of the words. Put a comma in place of that word.

1. The little puppy ate and played and slept.
2. The man found his shovel and dug a hole and planted the tree.
3. Giraffes and monkeys and lions were in the parade.

C. Write the answers to the questions.

Triff is a silly word for tree.

1. What is a triff?
2. Name a class that a triff is in.
3. What parts does a triff have?

D. Follow the directions.

1. First draw a triangle on your paper.
2. Then draw a rectangle around the triangle.
3. Then draw a circle next to the rectangle.
4. Then make a dot inside the circle.

STOP END OF LESSON 37.

A. Read each item. Write the direction that is more general.

1. Go to a store.
   Go to a pet store.

2. Wave to Roberto.
   Wave to a friend.

3. Hold up your left hand.
   Hold up your hand.

B. Write sentences about this picture.

1. Write two or more sentences about what you see in the picture.
2. Write one sentence about how the girl feels.

| steps | licking | happy | loves |

Independent Work

C. Write each sentence, but leave out one of the words. Put a comma in place of that word.

1. The healthy man ate peas and beans and corn.
2. They painted the car purple and green and orange.
3. Jim wants a picture of an elephant or a tiger or a lion.

D. Read about a torz. Write the answers to the questions.

A **torz** is a pet. It eats meat. A torz barks.
1. What is a torz?
2. How do you know that a torz is not a deer?
3. How do you know that a torz is not a cat?

E. Write synonyms and opposites.

1. Write the opposite of each word.
   a. narrow   b. inside   c. down

2. Write the synonym for each word.
   a. fast   b. sad   c. skinny

STOP END OF LESSON 38.

A. Read each item. Write the direction that is more general.

1. Stamp your left foot.
   Stamp your foot.

2. Borrow a tool.
   Borrow some scissors.

3. Draw a big spotted cow.
   Draw a cow.

B. Write sentences about this picture.

1. Write two or more sentences about what you see in the picture.
2. Write one sentence about how the boy feels.

skates	lucky	helmet	sidewalk	dizzy	stick

Independent Work

C. Write each sentence, but leave out one of the words. Put a comma in place of that word.

1. Our pig is fat and pink and friendly.
2. Mai-Li saw lions and monkeys and snakes at the zoo.
3. Joshua and Luis and Adam went into the house.

D. Read about a mersho. Write the answers to the questions.

A **mersho** is a farm animal that has four legs. It moos.
You drink milk that comes from a mersho.

1. What is a mersho?
2. How do you know that a mersho is not a tiger?
3. How do you know that a mersho is not a chicken?

E. Follow the directions.

1. First make a dot on your paper.
2. Then draw a triangle beside the dot.
3. Then draw a horizontal line below the dot and the triangle.
4. Then make a dot inside the triangle.

STOP END OF LESSON 39.

A. Read each item. Write the direction that is more general.

1. Read a newspaper.
   Read something.

2. Bring me the blue bucket.
   Bring me the blue container.

3. Buy a pair of shoes.
   Buy a pair of tennis shoes.

B. Write sentences about this picture.

1. Write two or more sentences about what you see in the picture.
2. Write one sentence about how the girl feels.

rope	mad	ground	swing	hurt

Independent Work

C. Read about a juggo. Write the answers to the questions.

> A **juggo** is a vehicle. It has two wheels, and you sit on it.
> A juggo has an engine.

1. What is a juggo?
2. How do you know that a juggo is not a car?
3. How do you know that a juggo is not a bicycle?

D. Write synonyms and opposites.

1. Write the opposite of each word.
   a. out   b. dirty   c. fat

2. Write the synonym for each word.
   a. glad   b. beautiful   c. little

E. Follow the directions.

1. First draw a circle on your paper.
2. Then make a dot in the middle of the circle.
3. Then draw a vertical line next to the circle.
4. Then draw a horizontal line above the whole thing.

F. Write each sentence, but leave out one of the words. Put a comma in place of that word.

1. Jacob will buy the hammer and the nails and the wood.
2. It was cold and dark and windy outside.
3. She wants to read a book or a magazine or a newspaper.

STOP END OF LESSON 40.

LESSON 41

A. Number your paper from 1 to 3. Rewrite each sentence to make the subject more specific. Circle the subject.

1. The tree is next to the house.
2. The tree is next to a car.
3. The car has a flat tire.

B. Write three or more sentences that tell what the boy will do.

| refrigerator | door | open | carton | milk | carry |

Independent Work

C. Write each sentence, but leave out one of the words. Put a comma in place of that word.

1. Molly will put away her bike and wagon and skateboard.
2. The sweater was soft and warm and cozy.
3. They had to shop for notebooks and pencils and markers.

D. Follow the directions.

1. First draw a rectangle on your paper.
2. Then draw a horizontal line inside the rectangle.
3. Then draw a circle next to the rectangle.
4. Then draw a triangle below the rectangle.

 END OF LESSON 41.

A. Number your paper from 1 to 3. Rewrite each sentence to make the subject more specific. Circle the subject.

1. The girl is smiling.
2. The girl is frowning.
3. The flowers are in a basket.

B. Write three or more sentences that tell what the woman will do.

front porch	box	house	inside	woman

Independent Work

C. Write sentences.

1. Write a sentence that asks a question about **that long pencil.**
2. Write a sentence that tells about **everybody.**

D. Follow the directions.

1. First draw a horizontal line on your paper.
2. Then make a dot above the middle of the horizontal line.
3. Then draw a rectangle below the middle of the horizontal line.
4. Then make a dot inside the rectangle.

E. Read each item. Write the direction that is more general.

1. Draw a farm animal.
   Draw a horse.

2. Take a picture of a bear.
   Take a picture of a wild animal.

3. Feed a cat.
   Feed a striped cat.

STOP END OF LESSON 42.

A. Number your paper from 1 to 3. Rewrite each sentence to make the subject more specific. Circle the subject.

1. The boy is wearing a white shirt.
2. The bike is next to the boy who is frowning.
3. The boy is sitting on a bike.

B. Write three or more sentences that tell what the woman will do.

woman	sweater	decide

dressing room

SWEATERS

Independent Work

C. Write three or more things that are in each class.

1. vehicles
2. containers
3. tools

D. Follow the directions.

1. First draw a horizontal line on your paper.
2. Then make a dot above the middle of the horizontal line.
3. Then draw a circle at one end of the horizontal line.
4. Then draw a circle at the other end of the horizontal line.

E. Read each item. Write the direction that is more general.

1. Eat some fruit.
   Eat some oranges.

2. Buy some chairs.
   Buy some furniture.

3. Call someone on the phone.
   Call José on the phone.

STOP END OF LESSON 43.

LESSON 44

A. Number your paper from 1 to 3. Rewrite each sentence to make the subject more specific.

1. A man is standing next to the window.
2. A man is talking to a woman.
3. A cat is under the table.

B. Write three or more sentences that tell what the girl will do.

hamburger	slices	tomato
ketchup	mustard	

Independent Work

C. Write sentences.

1. Write a sentence that asks a question about **Olivia's puppy.**
2. Write a sentence that tells about **those long boards.**

D. Read about a frizzo. Write the answers to the questions.

A **frizzo** is a tool. It has a blade. You use a frizzo when you eat.

1. What is a frizzo?
2. How do you know that a frizzo is not a shovel?
3. How do you know that a frizzo is not a spoon?

E. Read each item. Write the direction that is more general.

1. Go to the store on Green Street.
   Go to the store at 312 Green Street.

2. Pick up the things in your room.
   Pick up the shirts in your room.

3. Move the desks.
   Move the furniture.

STOP END OF LESSON 44.

67

A. Read the sentences. Then follow the instructions.

1. The cat was under the house.

   Write a sentence that is more general.

2. The animal was in the building.

   Write a sentence that is more specific.

B. Number your paper from 1 to 3. Rewrite each sentence to make the subject more specific.

1. The book is on the desk.
2. The book is in the dog's mouth.
3. The dog is barking.

C. Write three or more sentences that tell what the man will do.

toothbrush	toothpaste	teeth

Independent Work

D. Follow the directions.

1. First draw a vertical line on your paper.
2. Then draw a rectangle at the top of the vertical line.
3. Then make a dot in the middle of the rectangle.
4. Then draw a circle around the whole thing.

E. Write synonyms and opposites.

1. Write a synonym for each word.
   a. silent   b. over   c. large
2. Write the opposite of each word.
   a. thin   b. stop   c. empty

STOP END OF LESSON 45.

LESSON 46

A. Read the sentences. Then follow the instructions.

1. The candy is in the jar.

   Write a sentence that is more general.

2. The plant is next to the building.

   Write a sentence that is more specific.

B. Number your paper from 1 to 3. Rewrite each sentence to make the subject more specific.

1. The hat is on the table.
2. The woman is wearing a hat.
3. The woman is cooking dinner.

C. Number your paper from 1 to 6.
Write **true** or **false** for each statement.

1. Elephants talk on the telephone.
2. Elephants have trunks.
3. Horses have wheels.
4. Books have pages.
5. Tigers have stripes.
6. Horses drive cars.

D. Write three or more sentences that tell what the girl will do.

| water | tub | shampoo | wash | rinse |

Independent Work

E. Write sentences.

1. Write a sentence that tells about **his hat.**
2. Write a sentence that asks a question about **the ice-cream cone.**

F. Read each item. Write the direction that is more general.

1. Don't park in front of the building.
   Don't park in front of the school.

2. Open a box of crackers.
   Open a box.

3. Go into a kitchen.
   Go into a room.

STOP END OF LESSON 46.

A. Read the sentences. Then follow the instructions.

1. The girl lost the doll.

Write a sentence that is more general.

2. He put the vehicle in the building.

Write a sentence that is more specific.

B. Number your paper from 1 to 3. Rewrite each sentence to make the subject more specific.

1. The box is full.
2. The boy is holding a glass.
3. The boy is looking in a mirror.

C. Number your paper from 1 to 6.
Write **true** or **false** for each statement.

1. Cows eat trees.
2. Birds have wings.
3. Fish can swim.
4. Ice is hot.
5. Carrots are orange.
6. A mile is shorter than an inch.

D. Write three or more sentences that tell what the boy will do.

| recycle | bowl | food | can opener |

Independent Work

E. Follow the directions.

1. First draw a vertical line on your paper.
2. Then make a dot in the middle of the vertical line.
3. Then make a dot on one end of the vertical line.
4. Then make a dot on the other end of the vertical line.

F. Write three or more things that are in each class.

1. food
2. animals
3. plants

STOP END OF LESSON 47.

A. Number your paper from 1 to 3. Rewrite each sentence to make the subject more specific.

1. The car has girls in it.
2. The car is on the street.
3. The tree is next to the red car.

B. Read the sentences. Then follow the instructions.

1. The boy ate an orange.
   The boy ate outside.

   a. Write the sentence that tells **where** the boy ate.
   b. Write **where** he ate.
   c. Write the sentence that tells **what** the boy ate.
   d. Write **what** he ate.

2. The girl rode a horse.
   The girl rode in the park.

   a. Write the sentence that tells **where** the girl rode.
   b. Write **where** she rode.
   c. Write the sentence that tells **what** the girl rode.
   d. Write **what** she rode.

C. Number your paper from 1 to 5.
   Write whether each statement about the picture is **true** or **false.**

1. Three cats are running.
2. One cat is sitting.
3. All the animals are cats.
4. Two cats are lying on their backs.
5. Some of the cats are running.

D. Write three or more sentences that tell what the woman will do.

woman	girl's	hair dryer	comb	wash

Independent Work

E. Follow the directions.

1. First draw a triangle on your paper.
2. Then draw a rectangle around the triangle.
3. Then draw a circle next to the rectangle.
4. Then make a dot inside the circle.

F. Read the sentences. Then follow the instructions.

1. The girl dropped a hammer.

   Write a sentence that is more general.

2. The vehicle is under the plant.

   Write a sentence that is more specific.

 END OF LESSON 48.

A. Read each pair of sentences. Write the subject that is more specific. Then underline the word or words in the subject that tell more.

1. The boy ran.
   The short thin boy ran.

2. That green bottle broke.
   That bottle broke.

3. A dog bit me.
   A big brown dog bit me.

B. Read the sentences. Then follow the instructions.

1. He painted his wagon.
   He painted in the garage.
   a. Write the sentence that tells **where** he painted.
   b. Write **where** he painted.
   c. Write the sentence that tells **what** he painted.
   d. Write **what** he painted.

2. The horse ate in the barn.
   The horse ate hay.
   a. Write the sentence that tells **where** the horse ate.
   b. Write **where** it ate.
   c. Write the sentence that tells **what** the horse ate.
   d. Write **what** it ate.

C. Write whether each statement about the picture is **true** or **false**.

1. All the boys are wearing shoes.
2. Some of the boys are wearing shoes.
3. None of the boys are wearing socks.
4. Two boys are barefoot.
5. Two boys are wearing shoes and socks.

D. Write three or more sentences that tell what the boy will do.

tomatoes	basket

Independent Work

E. Write each sentence, but leave out one of the words. Put a comma in place of that word.

1. The boys washed the windows and the floors and the walls.
2. That woman will bring a cake or a pie or some cookies.
3. Roberto and Erin and Alex came along.
4. The puppy wagged its tail and barked and licked my face.

F. Read the sentences. Then follow the instructions.

1. The car ran into the house.

   Write a sentence that is more general.

2. The vehicle ran into a plant.

   Write a sentence that is more specific.

 END OF LESSON 49.

A. Look at each pair of sentences. Write the subject that is more specific. Then underline the word or words in the subject that tell more.

1. A fat green frog was jumping.
   A frog was jumping.

2. The car went fast.
   The red car went fast.

3. The little yellow bird is singing.
   The bird is singing.

B. Read the sentences. Then follow the instructions.

1. The man washed dishes.
   The man washed after lunch.
   a. Write the sentence that tells **when** the man washed.
   b. Write **when** he washed.
   c. Write the sentence that tells **what** the man washed.
   d. Write **what** he washed.

2. Those girls sang last night.
   Those girls sang many songs.
   a. Write the sentence that tells **when** those girls sang.
   b. Write **when** they sang.
   c. Write the sentence that tells **what** those girls sang.
   d. Write **what** they sang.

C. Write three or more sentences that tell what the man will do.

| corn | pot | water | stove | boiling |

Independent Work

D. Write whether each statement about the picture is **true** or **false**.

1. Some of the windows are open.
2. None of the windows are broken.
3. Three windows are closed.
4. One window is closed and broken.
5. Three windows are not broken.

E. Read the sentences. Then follow the instructions.

1. The person threw away the container.

    Write a sentence that is more specific.

2. The boy sat on the desk.

    Write a sentence that is more general.

 **STOP** END OF LESSON 50.

A. Make each sentence more specific by changing the predicate.

1. The woman is next to the car.
2. The man is next to the car.
3. The man will drive the car.

B. Copy the first sentence. Then write three or more sentences that tell what the man did.

coat	tie	shirt	took off	unbuttoned

The sun felt very hot.

Independent Work

C. Look at each pair of sentences. Write the subject that tells more.
   Underline the word or words in that subject that tell more.

   1. A fat green frog was jumping.
      A frog was jumping.

   2. The bird is singing.
      The little yellow bird is singing.

   3. This old car will not start.
      This car will not start.

D. Read the sentences. Then follow the instructions.

   1. She reads comic books.
      She reads in her bedroom.
      a. Write the sentence that tells **what** she reads.
      b. Write **what** she reads.
      c. Write the sentence that tells **where** she reads.
      d. Write **where** she reads.

   2. That woman was driving in the field.
      That woman was driving a tractor.
      a. Write the sentence that tells **where** that woman was driving.
      b. Write **where** she was driving.
      c. Write the sentence that tells **what** that woman was driving.
      d. Write **what** she was driving.

STOP END OF LESSON 51.

A. Make each sentence more specific by changing the predicate.

1. The girl has the ball.
2. The boy has the ball.
3. The dog is sitting next to the ball.

B. Copy the first sentence. Then write three or more sentences that tell what the girl did.

| girl | horse | saddle | climbed |

The girl wanted to ride her horse.

Independent Work

1. The boys are playing baseball.
   The boys are playing in the parking lot.
   a. Write the sentence that tells **where** the boys are playing.
   b. Write **where** they are playing.
   c. Write the sentence that tells **what** the boys are playing.
   d. Write **what** they are playing.

2. Laura was sewing a dress.
   Laura was sewing in her room.
   a. Write the sentence that tells **what** Laura was sewing.
   b. Write **what** she was sewing.
   c. Write the sentence that tells **where** Laura was sewing.
   d. Write **where** she was sewing.

D. Follow the directions.

1. First draw a rectangle on your paper.
2. Then draw a horizontal line below the rectangle.
3. Then draw a triangle below the middle of the horizontal line.
4. Then draw a horizontal line below the triangle.

E. Read each sentence. Then follow the instruction.

1. The person cooked his food.

   Write a sentence that is more specific.

2. The boy filled his cup.

   Write a sentence that is more general.

STOP END OF LESSON 52.

A. Make each sentence more specific by changing the predicate.

1. The woman is sitting in the chair.
2. The man is sitting in the chair.
3. The cat is scratching the chair.

B. Copy the first sentence. Then write three or more sentences that tell what the man did.

lightbulb	old	new	ladder

The man wanted to change a lightbulb.

Independent Work

1. Those oranges taste better.
   Those small oranges taste better.

2. His red rubber boots are on the porch.
   His boots are on the porch.

3. A lion jumped out of the bushes.
   A big lion jumped out of the bushes.

1. Those girls sang last night.
   Those girls sang at school.
   a. Write the sentence that tells **when** the girls sang.
   b. Write **when** they sang.
   c. Write the sentence that tells **where** the girls sang.
   d. Write **where** they sang.

2. We went swimming in the pond.
   We went swimming in the morning.
   a. Write the sentence that tells **when** we went swimming.
   b. Write **when** we went swimming.
   c. Write the sentence that tells **where** we went swimming.
   d. Write **where** we went swimming.

 END OF LESSON 53.

90

A. Complete each analogy.

1. A plane is to air as a boat is to _____ .

2. Driving is to a car as rowing is to a _____ .

3. A glass is to containers as a boat is to _____ .

4. A wheel is to a car as a sail is to a _____ .

5. A nail is to metal as a pencil is to _____ .

B. Copy the first sentence. Then write three or more sentences that tell what Doctor Booth did.

| cake | friends | bought | ice cream | called |

Doctor Booth

Doctor Booth planned her birthday party.

Independent Work

C. Make each sentence more specific by changing the predicate.

1. The man is washing.
2. The girl is washing.
3. The woman is washing.

D. Write whether each statement about the picture is **true** or **false.**

1. All the men have hair on their heads.
2. Some of the men have long hair.
3. Three of the men have short hair.
4. None of the men have hats.
5. Two men are bald.

E. Read the sentences. Then follow the instructions.

You will eat today.
You will eat soup.
    a. Write the sentence that tells **when** you will eat.
    b. Write **when** you will eat.
    c. Write the sentence that tells **what** you will eat.
    d. Write **what** you will eat.

 END OF LESSON 54.

A. Complete each analogy.

1. A school is to learning as a restaurant is to _____.

2. An apple is to red as a lemon is to _____.

3. Noisy is to loud as big is to _____.

4. A leg is to a chair as an eraser is to a _____.

5. A dog is to animals as a hammer is to _____.

B. Copy the first sentence. Then write three or more sentences that tell what the girl did.

bike	tire	air	helmet	flat	gas station

The girl got ready for a bike ride.

Independent Work

C. Make each sentence more specific by changing the predicate.

1. The cat is playing with a ball.
2. The dog is chewing a ball.
3. The baby is throwing a ball.

D. Follow the directions.

1. First draw a circle on your paper.
2. Then make a dot in the middle of the circle.
3. Then draw a triangle around the circle.
4. Then draw a circle around the triangle.

E. Read the sentences. Then follow the instructions.

1. The pigs ate all day long.
   The pigs ate some corn.
   a. Write the sentence that tells **when** the pigs ate.
   b. Write **when** they ate.
   c. Write the sentence that tells **what** the pigs ate.
   d. Write **what** they ate.

2. The boys rode horses.
   The boys rode yesterday.
   a. Write the sentence that tells **when** the boys rode.
   b. Write **when** they rode.
   c. Write the sentence that tells **what** the boys rode.
   d. Write **what** they rode.

STOP END OF LESSON 55.

A. Complete each analogy.

1. Fast is to slow as dry is to _____ .

2. A hammer is to tools as a flower is to _____ .

3. Sawing is to a saw as hammering is to a _____ .

4. A bird is to flying as a fish is to _____ .

5. A library is to books as a grocery store is to _____ .

B. Look at each pair of sentences. Write the predicate that tells more. Underline the word or words in that predicate that tell more.

1. A cat was sleeping.
   A cat was sleeping on the bed.

2. Those boys ate candy.
   Those boys ate candy before lunch.

3. The man hit the ball hard.
   The man hit the ball.

C. Copy the first sentence. Then write three or more sentences that tell what the man did.

| ceiling | ladder | cloth |
| floor | brush | |

The man wanted to paint the ceiling.

Independent Work

D. Write whether each statement about the picture is **true** or **false.**

1. Two cows have spots.
2. None of the cows have bells.
3. One spotted cow has a bell.
4. Some of the cows have spots.
5. All the cows are lying down.

E. Follow the directions.

1. First draw a horizontal line on your paper.
2. Then draw a rectangle above the horizontal line.
3. Then draw a triangle above the rectangle.
4. Then draw a dot inside the triangle.

 END OF LESSON 56.

A. Write whether each statement about the picture is **true** or **false** or **maybe.**

1. Some of the girls are wearing glasses.
2. The girl who is sitting is wearing glasses.
3. The girl who is sitting is named Jill.
4. All the girls are standing up.
5. Three girls are standing up.
6. Some of the girls did not eat breakfast.

B. Look at each pair of sentences. Write the predicate that tells more. Underline the word or words in that predicate that tell more.

1. The man spoke slowly and quietly.
   The man spoke.

2. The dog barked.
   The dog barked loudly.

3. We swam before lunch.
   We swam.

C. Copy the first sentence. Then write three or more sentences that tell what the boy did.

ointment	washed	bandage

The boy took care of his cut.

Independent Work

D. Complete each analogy.

1. A glove is to a hand as a shoe is to a ____.

2. Snow is to white as grass is to ____.

3. Fast is to slow as dry is to ____.

4. A hammer is to tools as a flower is to ____.

5. A boat is to the water as an airplane is to the ____.

E. Read the sentences. Then follow the instructions.

1. Jim was sleeping on the porch.
   Jim was sleeping after lunch.
   a. Write the sentence that tells **when** Jim was sleeping.
   b. Write **when** he was sleeping.
   c. Write the sentence that tells **where** Jim was sleeping.
   d. Write **where** he was sleeping.

2. The girls played on Monday.
   The girls played in the yard.
   a. Write the sentence that tells **when** the girls played.
   b. Write **when** they played.
   c. Write the sentence that tells **where** the girls played.
   d. Write **where** they played.

F. Read each sentence. Then follow the instruction.

1. The girls rode in a truck.
   Write a sentence that is more general.

2. The girl threw away her clothes.
   Write a sentence that is more specific.

STOP END OF LESSON 57.

A. Write whether each statement about the picture is **true** or **false** or **maybe.**

1. All the boys are standing up.
2. The boy with the coat is wearing a long-sleeved shirt.
3. Some of the boys are wearing short-sleeved shirts.
4. Two boys are wearing long-sleeved shirts.
5. None of the boys have money in their pockets.
6. The boy with the coat can run fast.

B. For each pair of sentences, write the sentence that tells more. Underline any words in that sentence that tell more.

1. The boy ate a banana.
   The little boy ate a banana.

2. The girl ran.
   The girl ran to the store.

3. The man sat.
   The man sat on an old chair.

4. A fat pig was eating.
   A pig was eating.

C. Copy the first sentence. Then write three or more sentences that tell what Julie did.

landed	swimsuit
diving board	water

Julie wanted to have fun.

Independent Work

D. Complete each analogy.

1. Fingers are to a hand as toes are to a _____.

2. A window is to glass as a pencil is to _____.

3. Hot is to cold as hard is to _____.

4. Yellow is to a banana as red is to an _____.

5. A container is to a can as a vehicle is to a _____.

E. Follow the directions.

1. First make a dot on your paper.
2. Then draw a vertical line through the dot.
3. Then draw a horizontal line through the dot.
4. Then draw a rectangle around the dot.

 **STOP** END OF LESSON 58.

103

A. For each pair of sentences, write the sentence that tells more. Underline any words in that sentence that tell more.

1. Two red balloons popped.
   Two balloons popped.

2. The bell rang.
   The bell rang for ten minutes.

3. A short boy ran away.
   A boy ran away.

4. He ate quickly.
   He ate.

B. Read the paragraph. Then write the answers to the questions.

1.   The girl had to stay in her room. She couldn't go out because she was sick. After supper, some of her friends came to visit her.
   a. **Who** is this paragraph about?
   b. **Where** did the girl have to stay?
   c. **Why** did she stay in her room?
   d. **When** did her friends visit her?
   e. **Who** visited her?

2.   Steve got a new bike at the store. He rode it all day Saturday. Then he let his sister ride it because he was tired.
   a. **Who** is this paragraph about?
   b. **What** did Steve get?
   c. **Where** did Steve get the bike?
   d. **When** did Steve ride the bike?
   e. **Why** did Steve let his sister ride the bike?

C. Copy the first sentence. Then write three or more sentences that tell what Gail did.

glue	dry	pieces
waited	picked	together

Gail fixed the broken dish.

Independent Work

D. Complete each analogy.

1. Top is to bottom as slow is to _____ .

2. A pen is to writing as a spoon is to _____ .

3. A bottle is to a container as a lion is to an _____ .

4. Green is to apples as yellow is to _____ .

E. Write whether each statement about the picture is **true** or **false** or **maybe.**

1. All the boys are sitting down.
2. None of the boys are swimming.
3. The boy with the hat is smiling.
4. The two boys eating ice cream are wearing hats.
5. The boy with the hat is talking.
6. The boy eating a hot dog is tall.

STOP END OF LESSON 59.

A. Read the paragraphs. Then write the answers to the questions.

1.　　　Bob went to the zoo yesterday. He went because he wanted to see the new baby monkeys. While he was there, he also saw a new baby elephant.

　　a. **Who** is this paragraph about?

　　b. **Where** did Bob go?

　　c. **Why** did Bob go to the zoo?

　　d. **When** did Bob go to the zoo?

　　e. **What** did Bob see at the zoo?

2.　　　Bill played in his house all morning. He stayed in the house because it was raining outside. In the afternoon, he went to Tom's house. Bill and Tom made paper airplanes.

　　a. **Who** is this paragraph about?

　　b. **Where** did Bill play all morning?

　　c. **Why** did Bill stay in the house?

　　d. **When** did Bill go to Tom's house?

　　e. **What** did Bill and Tom make?

B. Write quotations.

1.　　　Mike was riding the bus home from school. He got ready to get off the bus. Then the bus driver drove right by his house without stopping.

　　　　Write what you think Mike said.

2.　　　The boy was digging a deep hole in the yard. Suddenly, his shovel hit something hard. Water started shooting up out of the hole.

　　　　Write what you think the boy said.

C. Copy the first sentence. Then write three or more sentences that tell what Sally did.

umbrella	boots	raincoat	Sally

It was raining outside.

Independent Work

D. For each pair of sentences, write the sentence that tells more. Underline any words in that sentence that tell more.

1. He ate.
   He ate quickly.

2. The girls jumped into the lake.
   The girls jumped.

3. A beautiful red flower grows in the garden.
   A flower grows in the garden.

4. The children are sleeping.
   The children are sleeping under the tree.

E. Write whether each statement about the picture is **true** or **false** or **maybe.**

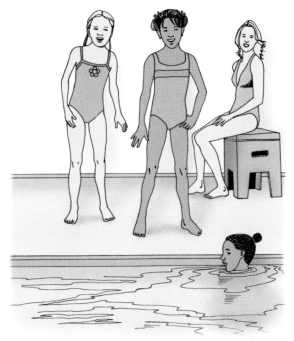

1. Some of the girls have on blue swimsuits.
2. One of the girls is in the water.
3. All the girls know how to swim.
4. Two of the girls are in the water.
5. The girl in the water has on a blue swimsuit.
6. The girl in the water is named Amber.

F. Complete each analogy.

1. A lemon is to yellow as lettuce is to _____ .

2. A nose is to smelling as an ear is to _____ .

3. A shirt is to clothing as a table is to _____ .

STOP END OF LESSON 60.

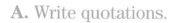

A. Write quotations.

1.   Tom worked for a man. The man walked up to Tom and said, "You are lazy."

Write what you think Tom said.

2.   John was in the house. It was nighttime. He was reading a book in his room. The electricity went out.

Write what you think John said.

3.   Shelly was on a horse named Rusty. They were crossing a stream. All at once, Rusty stopped right in the middle of the stream.

Write what you think Shelly said to Rusty.

B. Read both sentences in each item. Write a new sentence using the subject that tells more and the predicate that tells more.

1. A woman was laughing hard.
    A short woman was laughing.

2. The fat frog fell asleep.
    The frog fell asleep on the log.

3. Those monkeys played all afternoon.
    Those silly monkeys played.

4. His brother milked the brown cow.
    His big brother milked the cow.

C. Write two sentences about the man. Tell where the man is. Then tell what the man is doing.

rowing

boat

Independent Work

D. Read the sentences. Then follow the instructions.

1. The boy will paint tomorrow.
   The boy will paint the walls.
   a. Write the sentence that tells **when** the boy will paint.
   b. Write **when** he will paint.
   c. Write the sentence that tells **what** the boy will paint.
   d. Write **what** he will paint.

2. Mary ate ten bananas.
   Mary ate last night.
   a. Write the sentence that tells **when** Mary ate.
   b. Write **when** she ate.
   c. Write the sentence that tells **what** Mary ate.
   d. Write **what** she ate.

E. Write whether each statement about the picture is **true** or **false** or **maybe.**

1. All the men have beards.
2. Two men are frowning.
3. The man reading the newspaper has a beard.
4. All the men are wearing hats.
5. The man reading the newspaper is wearing glasses.
6. No men are standing up.

STOP END OF LESSON 61.

A. Read both sentences in each item. Write a new sentence using the subject that tells more and the predicate that tells more.

1. My new cup is full.
   My cup is full of milk.

2. A boy won the race today.
   A tall boy won the race.

3. The girl is warm and happy.
   The little girl is warm.

4. Five green turtles were swimming.
   Five turtles were swimming in the pond.

B. Write quotations.

1.   Bill was riding his new bike along the sidewalk. A boy came up to him, and said, "Hey. What are you doing with my bike?"

   Write what you think Bill said.

2.   Grace and her father were walking in the woods. All of a sudden, a voice said, "Hello. Who are you?"

   Write what you think Grace said.

3.   Sue was going to the garage to get her wagon. When she opened the garage door, a big dog started barking. Sue slammed the door shut.

   Write what you think Sue said.

C. Write two or more sentences about what you see in the picture. Then write one sentence about how the boy feels.

boat

river

afraid

rowing

Independent Work

D. Read the paragraph. Then follow the instructions.

Ann took a big cake to her grandma's house on Wednesday. She wanted to surprise her grandma because it was her grandma's birthday. Her grandma was very happy to get Ann's cake.

    a. Write **who** the story is about.
    b. Write **where** Ann went.
    c. Write **what** Ann took to her grandma.
    d. Write **why** Ann wanted to surprise her grandma.
    e. Write **who** was very happy.

E. Write each sentence, but leave out one of the words. Put a comma in place of that word.

    1. That girl ran and slipped and fell down.
    2. The girls drank milk and water and juice.
    3. Carol will buy carrots or beans or corn.

 **STOP** END OF LESSON 62.

A. Read both sentences in each item. Write a new sentence using the subject that tells more and the predicate that tells more.

1. The older girls are talking.
   The girls are talking about the dance.

2. Her pet snake was sleeping.
   Her snake was sleeping on the bed.

3. That girl sings funny songs.
   That happy girl sings.

4. Our new radio was playing.
   Our radio was playing too loudly.

B. Write three sentences. Write two sentences about the dog. Tell where the dog is. Tell what the dog is doing. Then tell how the woman feels.

| kitchen | eating | meat | mad |

Independent Work

C. Write quotations.

1.   Cindy was looking for her cat. She looked all over her house. Then she saw her father.

   Write what you think Cindy said to her father.

2.   Bill had nothing to do, so he walked over to Tom's house. Tom's mother answered the door.

   Write what you think Bill said to Tom's mother.

D. Read the paragraph. Then follow the instructions.

   Last summer, Mike painted the fence in back of his house. He painted the fence because his father asked him to paint it. Mike painted the fence green.

   a. Write **who** the story is about.
   b. Write **what** Mike painted.
   c. Write **where** Mike painted.
   d. Write **when** Mike painted the fence.
   e. Write **why** Mike painted the fence.
   f. Write **what color** Mike painted the fence.

STOP END OF LESSON 63.

A. Write one sentence with each verb. Do not use the same words in each sentence.

1. ran
2. will eat

3. is sleeping
4. was jumping

B. Write two or more sentences about what you see in the picture. Then write one sentence about how the boy feels.

wet	father	steps	marks	paint	sorry

Independent Work

C. Read both sentences in each item. Write a new sentence using the subject that tells more and the predicate that tells more.

1. This yellow bird sings.
   This bird sings all night long.

2. The tall boy can play.
   The boy can play very well.

3. Her monkey was driving her car.
   Her pet monkey was driving.

D. Write quotations.

1. Diana was hungry, but she had no money. She walked into a restaurant. Then she saw her friend Ted.
   Write what you think Diana said to Ted.

2. A big turtle was sleeping on the beach. Jamal thought the turtle was a rock. He sat down on it. The turtle started to move.
   Write what you think Jamal said.

E. Write three or more things that are in each class.

1. plants
2. animals
3. materials

STOP END OF LESSON 64.

A. Read the sentences.

Pair 1   They won't have food unless they go to the store.
Unless they go to the store, they won't have food.

Pair 2   They will go to the fair if they come on Tuesday.
If they come on Tuesday, they will go to the fair.

Pair 3   She sang a song while she brushed her hair.
While she brushed her hair, she sang a song.

B. Write one sentence with each verb. Do not use the same words in each sentence.

1. was digging   3. is singing
2. fell   4. kicked

C. Write two or more sentences about what you see in the picture. Then write one sentence about how the man feels.

surprised	paint	house	ladder	upset

119

Independent Work

D. Write quotations.

1.   Kevin was watching the tigers at the zoo. Suddenly, he saw that the cage door was open.

        Write what you think Kevin said.

2.   A dog chased Jill's cat up a tree. Jill wanted her cat to come down. But her cat was too scared.

        Write what you think Jill said.

E. Read both sentences in each item. Write a new sentence using the subject that tells more and the predicate that tells more.

1. The tiger is eating red meat.
   The big tiger is eating.

2. His older brother won.
   His brother won the big race.

3. The new red barn burned.
   The barn burned on Saturday.

STOP END OF LESSON 65.

A. Read the sentences.

Pair 1 My brother came home at noon.
At noon, my brother came home.

Pair 2 I had a bad cold on Tuesday.
On Tuesday, I had a bad cold.

Pair 3 Maria slept during the movie.
During the movie, Maria slept.

B. Write one sentence with each verb. Do not use the same words in each sentence.

1. are playing   3. are
2. will swim   4. laughed

C. Write two or more sentences about what you see in the picture. Then write one sentence about how the dog feels.

| suitcases | their car | trip | family | chasing | worried |

Independent Work

D. Read both sentences in each item. Write a new sentence using the subject that tells more and the predicate that tells more.

1. The bucket was full of nails.
   The rusty bucket was full.

2. Two frogs were sleeping in the sun.
   Two brown frogs were sleeping.

3. That short girl can jump.
   That girl can jump over the chair.

E. Read the sentences. Then follow the instructions.

1. The boys went sledding on the big hill.
   The boys went sledding this morning.

   a. Write the sentence that tells **when** the boys went sledding.
   b. Write **when** they went sledding.
   c. Write the sentence that tells **where** the boys went sledding.
   d. Write **where** they went sledding.

2. Jim fell on the ice.
   Jim fell last winter.

   a. Write the sentence that tells **when** Jim fell.
   b. Write **when** he fell.
   c. Write the sentence that tells **where** Jim fell.
   d. Write **where** he fell.

STOP END OF LESSON 66.

A. Write each sentence another way. Don't forget the comma.

1. I went to school every day.
2. The dogs are barking in the yard.
3. The students saved cereal boxes for their projects.

B. Write three or more sentences that tell what the woman will do to keep the cabin warm.

split	fireplace	wood	cabin	woman	ax

Independent Work

C. Write quotations.

1.   Kyra was walking in the park. She was getting tired, so she sat down on a bench. When she tried to get up, her dress stuck to the bench. The bench was covered with wet paint.
       Write what you think Kyra said.

2.   A man came to Cameron's house. He shook Cameron's hand and said, "You have won the big prize, Cameron. Here it is." The man put a rope in Cameron's hand. On the end of the rope was a real, live monkey.
       Write what you think Cameron said.

D. Write one sentence with each verb. Do not use the same words in each sentence.

1. is running
2. sat
3. will eat
4. was hopping

E. Write synonyms and opposites.

1. Write a synonym for each word.
   a. silent   b. over   c. large

2. Write the opposite of each word.
   a. thin   b. stop   c. empty

STOP END OF LESSON 67.

A. Write each sentence another way. Don't forget the comma.

1. It is warm inside the tent.
2. He wears his hat with his new coat.
3. We had turkey for Thanksgiving dinner.

B. Write three or more sentences that tell what Janet will do to celebrate her birthday.

candles	birthday	presents	friends	serve

Independent Work

C. Write one sentence with each verb. Do not use the same words in each sentence.

1. licked
2. can swim
3. will sleep
4. are running

125

D. Read both sentences in each item. Write a new sentence using the subject that tells more and the predicate that tells more.

1. A big black bug was eating.
   A bug was eating the leaf.

2. Those men were running in the park.
   Those old men were running.

3. His pants ripped in the back.
   His new pants ripped.

E. Write whether each statement about the picture is **true** or **false** or **maybe.**

1. All the monkeys have long tails.
2. All the monkeys are eating.
3. Two monkeys are hanging upside down.
4. The monkey with its back turned is eating an orange.
5. None of the monkeys are wearing hats.
6. The monkey that is hanging upside down loves peanuts.

 END OF LESSON 68.

126

A. Copy the first sentence. Then write three or more sentences that tell what Jim's dad will do.

Jim yelled at his dad.

| move | yelled | bicycle |

Independent Work

B. Write each sentence another way. Don't forget the comma.

1. Mary got a doll for her birthday.
2. He ripped his pants with the scissors.
3. I make my bed every morning.

C. Write one sentence with each verb. Do not use the same words in each sentence.

1. will run   3. are
2. was reading   4. hit

D. Write quotations.

1.   Chen-Li was very hungry. She made a big sandwich. She was just going to take a bite when her brother came in. He said, "That looks good. Let me have half."

    Write what you think Chen-Li said.

2.   Kristin was going to bed. She put on her pajamas. Then she pulled back the bedcovers. All of a sudden, she saw a big bug crawl across the sheets.

    Write what you think Kristin said.

E. Read the paragraph. Then follow the instructions.

    Mary went swimming in the lake before breakfast. She went swimming just for fun. While she was swimming, she saw some fish in the water.

    a. Write **who** the story is about.
    b. Write **where** Mary went swimming.
    c. Write **when** Mary went swimming.
    d. Write **why** Mary went swimming.
    e. Write **what** Mary saw in the water.

STOP END OF LESSON 69.

A. Copy the first sentence. Then write three or more sentences that tell what Sam did.

Sam was very hungry.

| frosting | cake | fingers | sorry |

Independent Work

B. Read both sentences in each item. Write a new sentence using the subject that tells more and the predicate that tells more.

1. That big balloon popped.
   That balloon popped in my face.

2. Two men opened the door of the spaceship.
   Two green men opened the door.

3. The wooden box was full.
   The box was full of money.

C. Write each sentence another way. Don't forget the comma.

1. You can see her house from the hill.
2. The dogs barked when we came home.
3. Every afternoon, she takes a nap.

D. Read the paragraph. Then follow the instructions.

Before school, Lori rode her bike to the grocery store. Lori went to the store because her mother needed some milk. After Lori got home from the store, she rode the bus to school.

a. Write **who** the paragraph is about.
b. Write **what** Lori went to the store to get.
c. Write **when** Lori went to the store.
d. Write **why** Lori went to the store.

E. Write each sentence, but leave out one of the words. Put a comma in place of that word.

1. Al will buy the hammer and the nails and the wood.
2. It was cold and dark and windy outside.
3. She wants to read a book or a magazine or a newspaper.

STOP END OF LESSON 70.

A. Write each sentence another way by moving words that are in the predicate.

1. Patrice went to the dentist every day last week.
2. The cows are resting in the pasture.
3. At parties, my brother always dances.

B. Write general sentences.

1.   Carlos put his backpack on the table. He took out a math book, an English book and a spelling book. He pulled out his pencil box and a notebook. He found a pencil in the pencil box and took three sheets of paper from the notebook. He pulled up a chair to the table and sat down.

    Write a general sentence that tells what Carlos did. Start with the word **Carlos.**

2.   Betty turned on the oven. She opened a box of cake mix and dumped its contents into a bowl. She added eggs and milk. Betty stirred the mixture and poured it into a pan. She put the pan in the hot oven and set the timer for 25 minutes.

    Write a general sentence that tells what Betty did. Start with the word **Betty.**

C. Write three or more sentences. Tell what happened **before** the boy saw that the floor was covered with water. Make the subject of each sentence **the boy, he, the water** or **the tub.** Then copy the sentence under the picture.

> toothbrush
>
> running
>
> bathtub

The boy saw that the floor was covered with water.

Independent Work

D. Complete each analogy.

    1. A cup is to a handle as a chair is to a _____ .

    2. A tire is to rubber as a belt is to _____ .

    3. Over is to under as in is to _____ .

    4. A knife is to cutting as a shovel is to _____ .

E. Write one sentence with each verb below.

    1. were talking   3. will climb

    2. is digging   4. are

STOP END OF LESSON 71.

132

LESSON 72

A. Write each sentence another way by moving words that are in the predicate.

1. Maggie got a doll for her birthday.
2. He cut the paper with the scissors.
3. Every morning, I make my bed.

B. Write general sentences.

1.   Dora and Belinda arrived at the gym. In the dressing room, they changed into their gym clothes. They walked into the gym and joined a group of girls who were doing stretching exercises. After spending an hour doing many different exercises, Dora and Belinda were very tired.

   Write a general sentence that tells what Dora and Belinda did. Start with the words **Dora and Belinda.**

2.   Sonia wheeled her bicycle to the backyard. She poured some soap into the bottom of the bucket and filled the bucket with water. She used a soapy sponge to scrub her bicycle. Then she used a hose to rinse off the soap. She let the bicycle dry in the sun.

   Write a general sentence that tells what Sonia did. Start with the word **Sonia.**

C. Write three or more sentences. Tell what happened **before** the girl fell and hurt her ankle. Make the subject of each sentence **the girl** or **she.** Then copy the sentence under the picture.

The girl fell and hurt her ankle.

| ice-skating | friends | frozen pond | ankle | stick |

Independent Work

D. Follow the directions.

1. First draw a horizontal line on your paper.
2. Then draw a vertical line through one end of the horizontal line.
3. Draw another vertical line through the other end of the horizontal line.
4. Then draw a circle above the horizontal line.

E. Write the answers to the questions.

Jukoz is a silly word for tree.

1. What is a jukoz?
2. Name a class that a jukoz is in.
3. What parts does a jukoz have?
4. What do you do with a jukoz?

STOP END OF LESSON 72.

A. Write each sentence another way by moving words that are in the predicate.

1. Inside the tent, it is warm.
2. With his new coat, he wears his hat.
3. We had turkey for Thanksgiving dinner.

B. Write general sentences.

1.   Luisa put some celery and tomatoes in her grocery cart. Then she went to the meat counter and chose some fish. She picked up a loaf of bread and some cans of soup. Then she went to the check-out counter. She paid for her things and left the store.

Write a general sentence that summarizes what Luisa did. Start with the word **Luisa.**

2.   Amy opened the garage door and got into her car. She started the engine and backed her car out of the garage. She closed the garage door, looked in her rearview mirror and backed onto the street. Then she started to drive her car to her office.

Write a general sentence that summarizes what Amy did. Start with the word **Amy.**

C. Write three or more sentences. Tell what happened **before** the man got out of his car. Make the subject of each sentence **the road, the car** or **the man.** Then copy the sentence under the picture.

The man got out of his car.

| icy road | steep hill | slid | driving |

Independent Work

D. Read both sentences in each item. Write a new sentence using the subject that tells more and the predicate that tells more.

1. That old house fell down.
   That house fell down five years ago.

2. A new flower came up.
   A flower came up in the garden.

3. Those girls were laughing at the clowns.
   Those little girls were laughing.

E. Complete each analogy.

1. A kitchen is to cooking as a bedroom is to ⬜.

2. A window is to glass as a magazine is to ⬜.

3. Food is to eating as a book is to ⬜.

4. Hard is to difficult as skinny is to ⬜.

5. A point is to a pencil as a wing is to a ⬜.

STOP END OF LESSON 73.

A. Write general sentences.

1.   Jimmy got out of bed, took a shower and put on his clothes. Then he went to the kitchen, sat down and ate breakfast. Then he picked up his homework papers, kissed his mom and said, "Good-bye." He opened the front door and ran down the steps.

   Write a general sentence that summarizes what Jimmy did.

2.   Reggie and Sam got out of the bus close to Cinema 8. They walked to the ticket counter and bought two tickets. They went into the lobby where they bought a big bag of popcorn. They walked into the dark movie theater and found good seats.

   Write a general sentence that summarizes what Reggie and Sam did.

B. Write three or more sentences. Tell what happened **before** the boys talked about what they should do. Make the subject of each sentence **the boys, the ball** or **someone.** Then copy the sentence under the picture.

The boys talked about what they should do.

baseball	window	house	someone

Independent Work

C. Write whether each statement about the picture is **true** or **false** or **maybe.**

1. None of the men have glasses.
2. Some of the men are bald.
3. One man is not smiling.
4. The man with glasses is bald.
5. Only two men are smiling.
6. One man is barefoot.

D. Read both sentences in each item. Write a new sentence using the subject that tells more and the predicate that tells more.

1. The dog fell asleep on my lap.
   The little brown dog fell asleep.

2. A tall man helped me.
   A man helped me fix my bike.

3. Those fat rabbits ate everything.
   Those rabbits ate everything in the garden.

STOP END OF LESSON 74.

A. Write general sentences.

1.   José picked up his bat and his glove. Barbara picked up the balls. They walked over to the park where they met their friends. José and Barbara chose sides so that each side had nine players. Then they went onto the playing field.

Write a general sentence that summarizes what José and Barbara did.

2.   Glen picked up the socks and pants that were on the floor and put them into the clothes basket. He made his bed. Then he picked up some paper bags and two paper plates. He took them to the kitchen and put them into the wastebasket under the sink.

Write a general sentence that summarizes what Glen did.

B. Write three or more sentences. Tell what happened **before** the dog ran out of the kitchen. Make the subject of each sentence **the woman, the bucket** or **the dog.** Then copy the sentence under the picture.

mopping

bucket

floor

tipped

yelled

The dog ran out of the kitchen.

Independent Work

C. Read the story. Then follow the instructions.

Last winter, Ted wanted to go sledding. But Ted did not have a sled. He was not very happy. Ted looked at the other boys sledding down the hill near his house.

Then Ted went home. "I will make a sled," he said. Ted found an old rocking chair. "This will make a good sled," he said. And it did make a good sled. Ted put the chair at the top of the hill and zoom, down the hill he went.

All the other boys said, "Ted's sled is the best sled of all."

a. Write **who** the story is about.
b. Write **where** Ted put the old rocking chair.
c. Write **when** the story took place.
d. Write **why** Ted got an old rocking chair.

STOP END OF LESSON 75.

A. Write general sentences.

1.   Maria and Darla went into the changing room to put on their swimsuits. Then they put their clothes in a locker. They went to the pool and jumped in. They swam, dived under the water and played catch with a large beach ball. At last they got out of the pool and rested in chairs near the pool.

Write a general sentence that summarizes what Maria and Darla did.

2.   Tino carried the tiny tree and a shovel to the backyard. Then he dug a hole. He put the tree into the hole and filled the hole with dirt so that the tree's roots were covered. He made sure the tiny tree was standing up straight. Then he got the hose and watered the tree.

Write a general sentence that summarizes what Tino did.

B. Write three or more sentences. Tell what happened **before** the girl pulled hard and the kite ripped. Make the subject of each sentence **the girl, the wind** or **the kite.** Then copy the sentence under the picture.

The girl pulled hard, and the kite ripped.

| flying | kite | ripped | wind | blew | strong |

Independent Work

C. Read this sentence: The **food** is in the **container.**

1. Write a sentence that tells what kind of **food** and what kind of **container.**
2. Write the sentence that tells more.

D. Write each sentence another way by moving words that are in the predicate.

1. After eating lunch, we took a nap.
2. Bob and Al were playing tag at school.
3. Jane started crying during the movie.

E. Follow the directions.

1. First draw a horizontal line on your paper.
2. Then draw a vertical line through the left end of the horizontal line.
3. Then draw a rectangle above the right end of the horizontal line.
4. Then draw a circle below the middle of the horizontal line.

STOP END OF LESSON 76.

A. Write each present-tense statement so that it is a past-tense statement. Write each past-tense statement so that it is a present-tense statement.

1. The birds were flying around the tree.
2. Tom is buying a new shirt.
3. You were eating lots of vegetables.

B. Write general sentences.

1.   Dimitri took some big pieces of paper from the bottom drawer of his desk. He found his box of paints. The brushes were inside the box. He took an empty jar and filled it with water. He put the paper, the box of paints and the jar of water on the kitchen table. Then he sat down and opened his paint box.

Write a general sentence that summarizes what Dimitri did.

2.   Nina opened the refrigerator. She took out a head of lettuce, two tomatoes and one cucumber. She put them in the sink and washed them. She peeled and sliced the cucumber, and then she sliced the tomatoes. She put these vegetables into a big bowl and added the leaves of lettuce. She used two big spoons to mix these vegetables together.

Write a general sentence that summarizes what Nina did.

C. Write three or more sentences. Tell what happened **before** the cowboy landed on the ground. Make the subject of each sentence **the cowboy, he** or **the horse.** Then copy the sentence under the picture.

The cowboy landed on the ground.

cowboy	horse	saddle	threw

Independent Work

D. Write quotations.

1.   Jean was fishing in the river. All at once, a big fish stuck his head out of the water. The fish said, "Go away. We don't want anyone fishing here."

   Write what you think Jean said.

2.   Steve was playing on the slide with his little brother Tyrone. Tyrone was sitting at the top of the slide. He was hanging on tight because he was afraid to slide down.

   Write what you think Steve said.    **STOP** END OF LESSON 77.

LESSON 78

A. Write each present-tense statement so that it is a past-tense statement. Write each past-tense statement so that it is a present-tense statement.

1. I am camping in the park.
2. They were playing baseball.
3. The horse is standing in the field.

B. Write general sentences.

1.   Manuel opened the big black case and took out his guitar. He tested each string to make sure it was in tune. He opened his notebook and read what his music teacher wanted him to do. He put his music book on the music stand. He opened the book and began to play.

   Write a general sentence that summarizes what Manuel did.

2.   Katie filled her glass with milk. She filled her salad bowl with salad and her dinner plate with corn, chicken and potatoes. She ate her meal and drank all her milk.

   Write a general sentence that summarizes what Katie did.

C. Write three or more sentences. Tell what happened **before** the man fell down. Make the subject of each sentence **the man, the cat, the dog** or **the leash.** Then copy the sentence under the picture.

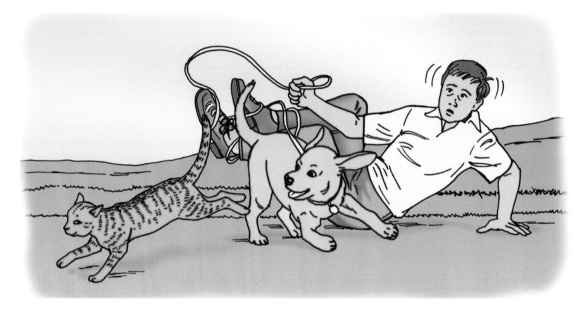

The man fell down.

around	leash	wrapped

Independent Work

D. Write each sentence another way by moving words that are in the predicate.

1. You can see her house from the hill.
2. The dogs barked when we came home.
3. Every afternoon, she takes a nap.

150

E. Write the answers to the questions.

Truff is a silly word for cup.

1. What is a truff?
2. Name a class that a truff is in.
3. What do you do with a truff?

F. Follow the directions.

1. First draw a circle on your paper.
2. Then draw a horizontal line through the middle of the circle.
3. Then draw a triangle below the left end of the horizontal line.
4. Then draw a rectangle above the right end of the horizontal line.

STOP END OF LESSON 78.

LESSON 79

A. Write each present-tense statement so that it is a past-tense statement. Write each past-tense statement so that it is a present-tense statement.

1. She was eating corn and peas.
2. Juan is swimming across the pool.
3. The bottle is full of milk.

B. Write general sentences.

1.   Joe, Brenda and Tim picked up some books and got into the car. Tim drove the car to a parking lot. They walked into the building where they put their books on the counter. Then Joe, Brenda and Tim looked for new books. They each found three books and checked them out.

   Write a general sentence that summarizes what Joe, Brenda and Tim did.

2.   Delia and her little sister put on hats, coats, boots and mittens. Delia opened the back door, and both girls went outside. First the girls made snowballs and threw them at the fence. Then they rolled up big balls and made a snowman. They used rocks and a stick to make the snowman's face.

   Write a general sentence that summarizes what Delia and her little sister did.

C. Write three or more sentences. Tell what happened **before** the man could not believe what he saw in the mirror. Make the subject of each sentence **the man, the barber** or **he.** Then copy the sentence under the picture.

The man could not believe what he saw in the mirror.

barber	decided	barbershop
mirror	haircut	shaved

Independent Work

D. Read the story. Then write the answers to the items.

One week ago, Mike got a magic ball. Every time Mike bounced it, the ball got bigger. At first, it was small. After Mike played with it for a day, the ball was as big as a basketball. After the second day, Mike's magic ball was as big as his room. So he had to leave it outside. After another day, it was as big as Mike's house. It was too big to play with. Poor Mike.

   a. Write **who** the story is about.

   b. Write **when** Mike got the magic ball.

   c. Write **where** Mike had to leave his ball.

   d. Write **why** Mike had to leave it outside.

STOP END OF LESSON 79.

A. Write each sentence, using contractions.

1. **He is** going to the store.
2. The boy **is not** wet.
3. She **can not** come.

B. Write general sentences.

1.   Hiroshi yawned and looked at the clock. He went to his bedroom and changed into his pajamas. Then he brushed his teeth in the bathroom. When he was done, he said good night to his parents and returned to his bedroom. He got into bed and turned out the light. He fell asleep quickly.

    Write a general sentence that summarizes what Hiroshi did.

2.   Carol went to the bookstore and looked at different books. She read a few pages of one that looked interesting, and then she bought it. She went back to her house, sat in her favorite chair and began to read. The book was about a girl who became a doctor. Carol read quickly. After a few hours, she closed the book and put it on her shelf.

    Write a general sentence that summarizes what Carol did.

C. Write three or more sentences. Tell what happened **before** the squirrel got mad at the man. Make the subject of each sentence **the man, he** or **the squirrel.** Then copy the sentence under the picture.

ax
tree
chopped

The squirrel got mad at the man.

Independent Work

D. Write each present-tense statement so that it is a past-tense statement. Write each past-tense statement so that it is a present-tense statement.

1. The boys were running around the track.
2. Jeffrey is painting a picture.
3. The boat is full of people.

E. Write each sentence another way by moving words that are in the predicate.

1. Amos read his book before he went to sleep.
2. Katie ate her apple after school.
3. When they finished mopping the floor, they sat down.

 **STOP** END OF LESSON 80.

156

A. Write each sentence with a contraction in place of the underlined words.

1. Mike <u>could not</u> lift the box.
2. <u>She will</u> miss the bus.
3. <u>I am</u> warm and happy.

B. Write each sentence with one of the joining words shown. Remember the comma just before the joining word.

1. She liked bananas   she hated carrots.   but   or

2. He had new shoes   he had a new hat.   but   and

3. Tomorrow we will go swimming   we   or   but
will go hiking.

C. Read this passage.

It was almost winter. The trees had lost their leaves. As they walked to school, Mark and Ellie talked about what they would do Saturday.

Mark said, "I think we should go to Spirit Lake. We would have a very good time."

Ellie said, "But that's way up in the mountains. It's going to be like winter up there. I don't think that would be any fun."

Mark laughed and said, "Fun? It would be lots of fun. It should be beautiful up there. I'm going to bring my camera and take pictures."

"Maybe you're right," Ellie said.

D. Write a story about the picture. Tell what happened just before the picture. Tell what happened in the picture. Tell what the people said. Tell what happened next. Write all the sentences in the past tense.

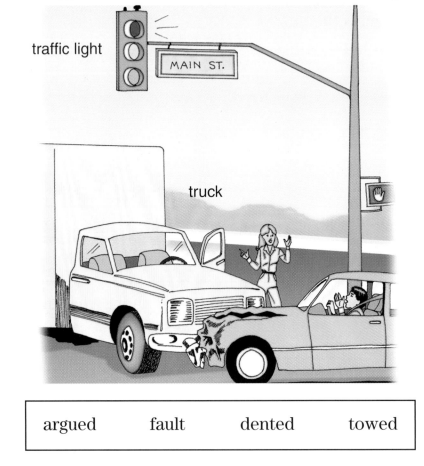

traffic light

MAIN ST.

truck

argued	fault	dented	towed

Independent Work

E. Write each present-tense statement so that it is a past-tense statement. Write each past-tense statement so that it is a present-tense statement.

1. Tom is buying a new shirt.
2. Yoko paints with a brush.
3. He was working hard.

F. Write whether each statement about the picture is **true, false** or **maybe.**

1. None of the rabbits are eating carrots.
2. One of the rabbits belongs to Mr. Jones.
3. Three of the rabbits love to eat lettuce.
4. The big rabbit loves to eat lettuce.
5. The big rabbit is not eating.

G. Write the abbreviation for each word.

1. Doctor
2. inch
3. hour
4. Street

 END OF LESSON 81.

A. Write each sentence **without** using a contraction.

1. They weren't sweeping the floor.
2. My sister wasn't at school.
3. You're standing on my foot.

B. Write each sentence with one of the joining words shown. Remember the comma just before the joining word.

1. The bike was old   it was rusty.   and   or

2. Greg and Don went to the lake   they fished   and   but for two hours.

3. The truck couldn't stop   it ran into a tree.   and   but

C. Read this passage.

    Hector and Maria took turns riding in a swing during recess. First Hector rode in the swing. Then Maria took a turn. She stayed in the swing for a long time.

    Hector said, "Now it's my turn to ride the swing again." He thought Maria's turn should be over.

    Maria said, "Can I swing just a minute longer?" She was having so much fun.

    "I'll wait for you to finish," said Hector. He sat down on a bench.

    "Thank you," answered Maria.

    Just then, the bell rang. Recess was over. Maria said, "You can swing first tomorrow."

D. Write a story about the picture. Tell what happened just before the picture. Tell what happened in the picture. Tell what the people said. Tell what happened next. Write all the sentences in the past tense.

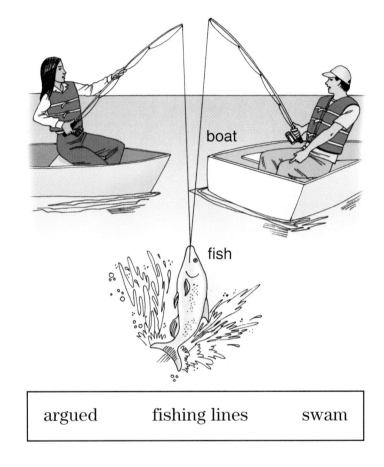

boat

fish

argued	fishing lines	swam

Independent Work

E. Write each sentence another way by moving words that are in the predicate.

1. Every Tuesday, I go swimming.
2. Bob fixed the car after dinner.
3. In the house, everyone was asleep.
4. His sister was sick on Monday and Tuesday.

F. Read the paragraph and follow the directions.

Al's father decided to build an electric car. After working a long time, he finished. One Saturday afternoon, Al's father called everyone outside. He got in his electric car and turned it on. First it went BANG! Then it went CLUNK! The electric car started going around in circles. Everyone ran into the house. Finally, the car crashed into the side of the house. Al's father got out of the car. He decided not to build another car.

a. Write **who** built the electric car.

b. Write **where** the electric car crashed.

c. Write **when** Al's father called everyone outside.

d. Write **why** everyone ran into the house.

e. Copy the general sentence that best summarizes what the paragraph is about.
- Al's father built an electric car.
- Al's father's electric car scared everyone.
- Al's father's car was not a good idea.

G. Write the word for each abbreviation.

1. Dr.
2. Mr.
3. yd.
4. mi.

STOP END OF LESSON 82.

A. Write each sentence **without** using a contraction.

1. You shouldn't walk on the ice.
2. I'm tired of walking.
3. He's climbing the apple tree.

B. Write each sentence with one of the joining words shown. Remember the comma just before the joining word.

1. She will go to the mall ___ she will go to my house.   but   or

2. Holly and her mother sang ___ they did not sing well.   but   or

3. Mike was thirsty ___ he looked all around for water.   and   but

C. Write a story about the picture. Tell what happened just before the picture. Tell what happened in the picture. Tell what the people said. Tell what happened next. Write all the sentences in the past tense.

dock

Don

canoe

tied

lake

paddled

Independent Work

D. Write the abbreviation for each word.

1. Mister	5. inch
2. hour	6. yard
3. foot	7. mile
4. Street	8. Doctor

E. Write each present-tense statement so that it is a past-tense statement. Write each past-tense statement so that it is a present-tense statement.

1. I am fixing your wagon.
2. The bathwater is very hot.
3. They were playing in the snow.

F. Read the paragraph and follow the directions.

Mary got a new puppy named Flash. When Mary went to school on Monday, she left Flash in her bedroom. Flash started to chew things up. First he chewed up Mary's new dress. After that, he messed up the bed and chewed up the rug. When Mary got back from school, she was very mad. Now Flash stays in the backyard when Mary is at school.

a. Write **who** got a new puppy.
b. Write **where** she left Flash.
c. Write **what** Flash chewed up first.
d. Write **when** Mary left Flash in her bedroom.
e. Copy the general sentence that best summarizes what the paragraph is about.
   • Mary's dog chewed up many things and made her mad.
   • Flash messed up the bed and chewed up the rug.
   • When Mary got back from school, she was mad.

 **STOP** END OF LESSON 83.

A. For sentences 1 through 4, say the word **walk.** For sentences 5 through 7, say the word **walks.** Repeat with **run** or **runs** and **jump** or **jumps.**

1. I _____ on sand.

2. You _____ on sand.

3. We _____ on sand.

4. They _____ on sand.

5. He _____ on sand.

6. She _____ on sand.

7. It _____ on sand.

B. Write each sentence with one of the joining words shown. Remember the comma just before the joining word.

1. It was cold _____ the bear did not feel cold.   or   but

2. She hurt her arm _____ she had a sore knee.   and   but

3. She didn't go home _____ she wasn't in school.   or   but

165

C. Write a story about the picture. Tell what happened just before the picture. Tell what happened in the picture. Tell what the people said. Tell what happened next. Write all the sentences in the past tense.

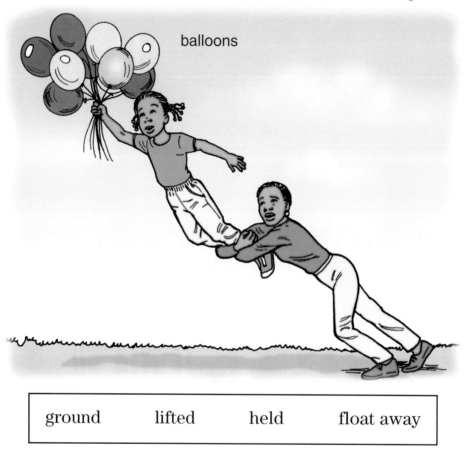

balloons

| ground | lifted | held | float away |

Independent Work

D. Write each sentence another way by moving words that are in the predicate.

1. After eating, my father takes a nap.
2. In the box, you will find a surprise.
3. The swimming pool opened last week.
4. Behind those trees, there is a lake.

E. Read the paragraph and follow the directions.

      Grace lived in a little house in the country. She was very lonely. Last summer, a big storm blew and blew around her house. The storm blew Grace and her house away. They sailed through the air. When the house came down, it was in a big city. Now there are lots of people around the house. Grace isn't lonely anymore.

    a. Write **who** the story is about.

    b. Write **where** the storm blew Grace's house.

    c. Write **when** the storm blew Grace's house away.

    d. Write **why** Grace isn't lonely anymore.

    e. Copy the sentence that best summarizes what the paragraph is about.

- A big storm blew Grace's house from the country to the city.
- Grace lived in a little house in the country.
- A big storm came last summer.

F. Write each sentence **without** using a contraction.

1. I'm tired of walking.
2. They weren't sweeping the floor.
3. You're standing on my foot.

STOP END OF LESSON 84.

A. For sentences 1 through 4, say the word **like.** For sentences 5 through 7, say the word **likes.** Repeat with **love** or **loves** and **sell** or **sells.**

---

1. I ▢ pictures.

2. You ▢ pictures.

3. We ▢ pictures.

4. They ▢ pictures.

---

5. He ▢ pictures.

6. She ▢ pictures.

7. It ▢ pictures.

B. Write each sentence with one of the joining words shown. Remember the comma just before the joining word.

1. We will wash the car ▢ we will not wax it.   but   and

2. The door was open ▢ cold air came inside.   or   and

3. Frank was lazy ▢ his sister worked hard.   but   or

C. Write a story about the picture. Tell what happened just before the picture. Tell what happened in the picture. Tell what the people said. Tell what happened next. Write all the sentences in the past tense.

sign

speeding ticket

police officer

| speed limit | driving |

Independent Work

D. Write each sentence with a contraction in place of the underlined words.

1. <u>They have</u> seen the circus before.
2. The clown <u>was not</u> very funny.
3. <u>She will</u> plant flowers here.

E. Write whether each statement about the picture is **true** or **false** or **maybe.**

1. None of the dogs are wearing a hat.
2. All the dogs have big ears.
3. Some of the dogs are big.
4. The dog with a hat chases cars.
5. All the small dogs have big ears.

F. Write the abbreviation for each word.

1. foot
2. Street
3. inch
4. Mister

 **STOP** END OF LESSON 85.

A. For sentences 1 through 4, say the word **pick.** For sentences 5 through 7, say the word **picks.** Repeat with **buy** or **buys** and **peel** or **peels.**

---

1. I ____ oranges.

2. You ____ oranges.

3. We ____ oranges.

4. They ____ oranges.

---

5. He ____ oranges

6. She ____ oranges.

7. It ____ oranges.

B. Write a story about the picture. Tell what happened just before the picture. Tell what happened in the picture. Tell what the people said. Tell what happened next. Write all the sentences in the past tense.

flat tire

driveway

changed

blocked

171

Independent Work

C. Write each sentence **without** using a contraction.

1. Our car didn't start this morning.
2. The horse couldn't pull the wagon.
3. She'll help fix my bike.

D. Write each sentence another way by moving words that are in the predicate.

1. Before lunch, we should make our beds.
2. There are ten monkeys in that cage.
3. After taking a nap, she can play.
4. The movie was crowded last night.

E. Write each present-tense statement so that it is a past-tense statement. Write each past-tense statement so that it is a present-tense statement.

1. The dog is eating the bone.
2. They were riding bikes.
3. One boy was sick.

F. Write one sentence with each verb below.

1. is   3. cut
2. was washing   4. will cook

G. Write the abbreviation for each word.

1. hour   3. inch
2. Doctor   4. yard

STOP END OF LESSON 86.

A. Write a story about the picture. Tell what happened just before the picture. Tell what happened in the picture. Tell what the people said. Tell what happened next. Write all the sentences in the past tense.

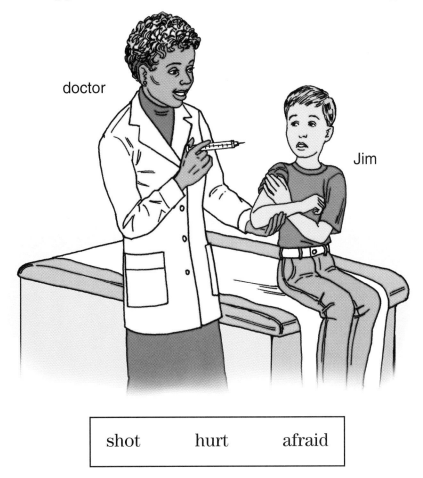

doctor

Jim

| shot | hurt | afraid |

Independent Work

B. Write the abbreviation for each word.

1. Doctor
2. Street
3. foot
4. yard
5. hour
6. inch
7. Mister
8. mile

C. Write the answers to the questions.

>   *Ragam* is a silly word for a garbage can.

1. What is a ragam?
2. Name a class that a ragam is in.
3. What do you do with a ragam?
4. What parts does a ragam have?

D. Read the paragraph and follow the directions.

>   For her birthday, Ellie got a strange doll. The doll looked just like other dolls, but it did something very strange. It walked around at night after everyone was asleep. Ellie would put the doll beside her on the bed every night. The next morning, the doll was always on the floor beside the bed. It had been out walking during the night. Ellie's bed was just too high for the doll to climb back up.

>   a. Write **who** got a strange doll.
>   b. Write **when** Ellie got the doll.
>   c. Write **where** Ellie put her doll every night.
>   d. Write **why** the doll was not in bed in the morning.
>   e. Copy the general sentence that best summarizes what the paragraph is about.
>
>   - Ellie got a doll for her birthday.
>   - Ellie's bed was too high for the doll to climb back up.
>   - Ellie had a strange doll that walked around at night.

STOP END OF LESSON 87.

A. Write a story about the picture. Tell what happened just before the picture. Tell what happened in the picture. Tell what the people said. Tell what happened next. Write all the sentences in the past tense.

amusement park	begged	frightened

Independent Work

B. Write each sentence another way by moving words that are in the predicate.

1. Every day, he reads the newspaper.
2. On top of the counter, there is some candy.
3. We have lots of fun at school.
4. After work, my father is tired.

C. For each pair of sentences: Write the sentence that tells more. Underline any words in that sentence that tell more.

1. The fire is burning the forest.
   The fire is burning.

2. That girl can swim.
   That girl can swim across the river.

3. This green plant smells good.
   This plant smells good.

D. Write one sentence with each verb below.

1. will jump   3. bit
2. is smiling   4. were throwing

E. Write each sentence with a contraction in place of the underlined words.

1. <u>They have</u> broken the clock.
2. The movie <u>is not</u> over yet.
3. <u>I will</u> call you later.

F. Write each present-tense statement so that it is a past-tense statement. Write each past-tense statement so that it is a present-tense statement.

1. Those people are shouting.
2. His feet were too big.
3. That man is very tall and thin.

STOP END OF LESSON 88.

A. Write one sentence with each simple subject.

1. rabbits   3. Bob
2. apples   4. Carol

B. Rewrite the paragraph in the past tense.

      Lizzie is a happy girl. She is packing a picnic lunch. Her mother is taking her to the mountains.

C. Write a story about the picture. Tell what happened just before the picture. Tell what happened in the picture. Tell what the people said. Tell what happened next. Write all the sentences in the past tense.

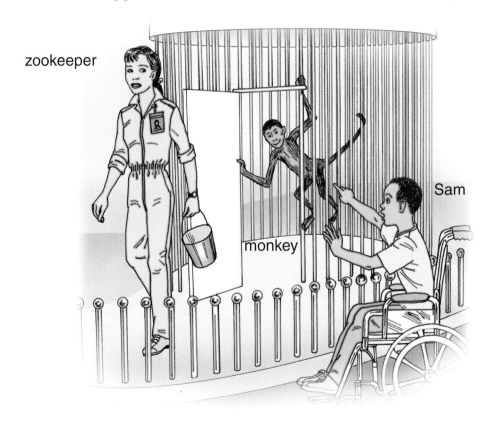

zookeeper

monkey

Sam

| cage | around | escape |

Independent Work

D. Rewrite each present-tense statement so that it is a past-tense statement. Rewrite each past-tense statement so that it is a present-tense statement.

1. Our teacher is very helpful.
2. The cats were chasing the birds.
3. You are spilling the water.

E. Write each sentence another way by moving words that are in the predicate.

1. After eating, the cat went to sleep.
2. In her purse, she has lots of coins.
3. It always snows in December.
4. In this cave, there is a treasure.

F. Read both sentences in each item. Write a new sentence using the subject that tells more and the predicate that tells more.

1. The man spoke slowly and quietly.
   The young man spoke.

2. The brown dog barked.
   The dog barked loudly.

3. The girls swam before lunch.
   The tall girls swam.

G. Write the abbreviation for each word.

1. Mister
2. mile
3. Street
4. inch
5. hour

 **STOP** END OF LESSON 89.

A. Write one sentence with each simple subject.

    1. man   3. dog

    2. bike   4. lions

B. Rewrite the paragraph in the present tense.

      The horse was running out of the barn. The farmer was throwing water on the barn. The barn was on fire.

C. Write a story about the picture. Tell what happened just before the picture. Tell what happened in the picture. Tell what the people said. Tell what happened next. Write all the sentences in the past tense.

washing	drying	swept	careful	broke

Independent Work

D. Read the paragraph and follow the directions.

Keiko went to her grandma's house last week. Her grandma was not home. Keiko thought, "I'll go into the house and surprise Grandma when she comes home." Keiko tried to open the door, but it was locked. So she opened a window. Just as Keiko got halfway through the window, it slowly slid down on top of her. She tried and tried to wiggle out, but she couldn't. She was stuck. Her grandmother came home and opened the window.

a. Write **who** the story is about.

b. Write **where** the story took place.

c. Write **when** the story took place.

d. Write **why** Keiko tried to climb through the window.

e. Copy the general sentence that best summarizes what the paragraph is about.

- Keiko tried to get in her grandma's house when she wasn't home.
- Keiko got stuck in the window when she tried to get into her grandma's house.
- The door was locked, so Keiko opened a window.

E. For each pair of sentences, write the sentence that tells more. Underline any words in that sentence that tell more.

1. Mary was talking.
   Mary was talking to Emma.

2. The tomato plants need water.
   The plants need water.

3. Her horse fell down the hill.
   Her horse fell.

 **STOP** END OF LESSON 90.

180

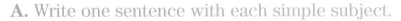

LESSON 91

A. Write one sentence with each simple subject.

1. toy   3. we
2. he   4. they

B. Write a story about the picture. Tell what happened just before the picture. Tell what happened in the picture. Tell what the people said. Tell what happened next. Write all the sentences in the past tense.

| hike | caught | pulled | finish |

Independent Work

C. Follow the directions.

1. First draw a horizontal line on your paper.
2. Then make a number 2 above the left end of the line.
3. Then make a number 5 above the right end of the line.
4. Then draw a triangle below the middle of the line.

D. Read the paragraph and follow the directions.

John lived on top of a high mountain. Yesterday, John's mother and father gave him a new bicycle. John went outside to try it out. He started riding down the mountain. He rode faster and faster. Soon he was far from home. He tried to stop, but he was going too fast. John couldn't stop until he got to the bottom of the mountain. He was a long way from home.

    a. Write **who** the paragraph is about.

    b. Write **where** John lived.

    c. Write **when** the story took place.

    d. Write **why** John couldn't stop.

    e. Copy the general sentence that best summarizes what the paragraph is about.

        • John rode his new bike far from home.

        • John got a new bike from his parents.

        • John stopped when he got to the bottom of the mountain.

E. Write each sentence another way by moving words that are in the predicate.

1. When I laugh, my stomach hurts.
2. That phone rings every five minutes.
3. There is an apple pie on that shelf.
4. In his pocket, he has a frog.

 **STOP** END OF LESSON 91.

182

A. Write one sentence with each simple subject.

1. desk
2. rabbits
3. Bob
4. ship

B. Write a story about the picture. Tell what happened just before the picture. Tell what happened in the picture. Tell what the people said. Tell what happened next. Write all the sentences in the past tense.

rope

line

| tug-of-war | team | yelled | pulled |

Independent Work

C. Write the abbreviation for each word.

1. Street	3. mile	5. Doctor	7. Mister
2. foot	4. inch	6. yard	8. hour

D. Complete each analogy.

1. A bag is to a container as a shovel is to a _____ .

2. Cutting is to a knife as painting is to a _____ .

3. Long is to short as narrow is to _____ .

4. A tomato is to red as snow is to _____ .

5. An elephant is to a jungle as a cow is to a _____ .

E. Write each sentence with a contraction in place of the underlined words.

1. The boys <u>are not</u> cutting the grass.
2. <u>You will</u> have to stand in line.
3. The little girl <u>could not</u> reach the carrots.

STOP END OF LESSON 92.

A. Write one sentence with each simple subject.

1. birds
2. she
3. snake
4. they

B. Write a story about the picture. Tell what happened just before the picture. Tell what happened in the picture. Tell what the people said. Tell what happened next. Write all the sentences in the past tense.

| ladder | children | branch | looked | called |

Independent Work

C. Read the paragraph and follow the directions.

Alma went to the movie on Saturday afternoon. She sat near the front of the theater to see better, but the movie wasn't very good. Alma began to feel sleepy. She shut her eyes. Suddenly, she woke up. The movie was over, and everyone was gone. She was the only person in the movie theater. Alma ran outside. It was dark.

a. Write **who** the story is about.
b. Write **when** Alma went to the movie.
c. Write **where** Alma sat.
d. Copy the general sentence that best summarizes what the paragraph is about.
- The movie wasn't very good.
- Alma sat near the front of the theater to see better.
- Alma fell asleep at the movie and slept a long time.

D. Write each sentence another way by moving words that are in the predicate.

1. After playing basketball, we took a shower.
2. We saw the city from the top of the building.
3. By August, the grass will turn brown.

E. Write each present-tense statement so that it is a past-tense statement. Write each past-tense statement so that it is a present-tense statement.

1. The cat is sitting on the refrigerator.
2. The new lamp was broken.
3. Those animals are getting hungry.

 END OF LESSON 93.

A. Write one sentence with each simple subject.

1. sandwich   3. Ted
2. he   4. tigers

B. Write a story about the picture. Tell what happened just before the picture. Tell what happened in the picture. Tell what the people said. Tell what happened next. Write all the sentences in the past tense.

| Mr. Jones | Mrs. Jones | engine | broke down | melt |

Independent Work

C. Write each sentence **without** using a contraction.

1. Bill didn't eat very much.
2. They're tired of playing baseball.
3. The girls weren't at school.

D. Write the paragraph so that it is a present-tense paragraph.

Casey was very lazy today. He was sitting under the apple tree. He was watching the apples fall.

E. Complete each analogy.

1. A forest is to a tree as a garden is to a _____ .
2. Pedaling is to a bike as rowing is to a _____ .
3. A chair is to furniture as a car is to _____ .
4. A pin is to metal as a baseball glove is to _____ .
5. A trunk is to a tree as a heel is to a _____ .

F. Read both sentences in each item. Write a new sentence using the subject that tells more and the predicate that tells more.

1. The skinny little rabbit jumped.
   The rabbit jumped out of the garden.

2. Her sister fell off the horse.
   Her older sister fell.

STOP END OF LESSON 94.

A. Write one sentence with each simple subject.

1. father
2. we
3. girls
4. I

B. Write a story about the picture. Tell what happened just before the picture. Tell what happened in the picture. Tell what the people said. Tell what happened next. Write all the sentences in the past tense.

umpire

Jenna

baseball	home plate	catcher

Independent Work

1. First write the letter **Z** on your paper.
2. Then draw a circle below the letter **Z.**
3. Then write the number 4 above the letter **Z.**
4. Then write the letter **T** inside the circle.

1. Alex <u>is not</u> eating his peas.
2. <u>I will</u> get the ice cream.
3. <u>They have</u> seen that movie.

Last Sunday, Kyle went to the park with his family. A man was selling balloons at the park. Kyle just loved balloons. First Kyle's mother bought him a balloon. Then his grandma bought him a balloon. Next his father bought him a balloon. His brother, his sister and his uncle bought him balloons. Kyle had so many balloons in his hand that he started to rise into the air. Soon he was floating high over the treetops.

a. Write **when** the story took place.
b. Write **where** Kyle went with his family.
c. Write **who** gave Kyle the first balloon.
d. Write **why** Kyle started to rise up into the air.
e. Copy the general sentence that best summarizes what the paragraph is about.
   - Kyle went to the park with his family.
   - Kyle's sister bought him a balloon, and so did his brother.
   - Kyle got so many balloons at the park that he floated away.

STOP END OF LESSON 95.

A. Write a story about the picture. Tell what happened just before the picture. Tell what happened in the picture. Tell what the people said. Tell what happened next. Write all the sentences in the past tense.

wish	candles

Independent Work

B. Complete each analogy.

1. An egg is to a chicken as milk is to a ⬚ .
2. Good is to bad as inside is to ⬚ .
3. Fur is to a dog as feathers are to a ⬚ .

C. Write the abbreviation for each word.

1. inch   3. Doctor
2. Mister   4. yard

D. Write one sentence with each simple subject.

1. Ann   3. hammer
2. rocks   4. she

E. Write each sentence **without** using a contraction.

1. The lion didn't get out of the cage.
2. She'll help you wash the dishes.
3. You've worked very hard.

STOP END OF LESSON 96.

A. Write a story about the picture. Tell what happened just before the picture. Tell what happened in the picture. Tell what the people said. Tell what happened next. Write all the sentences in the past tense.

Rachel

Frank

| trumpet | loud | music | sounded |

Independent Work

B. Write the paragraph so that it is a past-tense paragraph.

      Emma and Troy are feeling hot and tired. They are pulling weeds in the garden. The sun is very hot.

C. Write each sentence another way by moving words that are in the predicate.

1. To start the motor, you pull that rope.
2. We will go camping every summer.
3. On the other side, there is a swimming pool.

D. Read the paragraph and follow the directions.

Mike had a raft. Last Saturday, Mike decided to catch some fish. He put on his life jacket. He put the paddle and his fishing gear on the raft. He used the paddle to push the raft along in the water. He saw some fish jumping out of the water. To get close to the fish, Mike used the paddle to give his raft a big push. Then he dropped his fishing line into the water. The fish swam away. Mike didn't catch any fish that day.

a. Write **who** the story is about.
b. Write **when** Mike was on his raft.
c. Write **what** Mike used to push the raft along.
d. Write **why** Mike didn't catch any fish.
e. Copy the general sentence that best summarizes what the paragraph is about.
   • Mike used his raft to go fishing.
   • Mike pushed his raft with a paddle.
   • Mike saw some fish jumping out of the water.

STOP END OF LESSON 97.

A. Write a story about the picture. Tell what happened just before the picture. Tell what happened in the picture. Tell what the people said. Tell what happened next. Write all the sentences in the past tense.

| math | test | teacher | worried |

Independent Work

B. Write one sentence with each simple subject.

1. turtle
2. dime
3. Janet
4. dolls

C. Follow the directions.

1. First write the letter **M** on your paper.
2. Then draw a vertical line to the right of the letter **M.**
3. Then write the number **3** to the right of the vertical line.
4. Then draw a rectangle above the number **3.**

D. Complete each analogy.

1. A shovel is to digging as a hammer is to _____ .

2. Salt is to white as a carrot is to _____ .

3. Clothing is to a shirt as container is to a _____ .

4. A trunk is to a tree as a stem is to a _____ .

E. Write each statement another way by moving words that are in the predicate.

1. To keep warm, he got another blanket.
2. On Wednesday, the library is closed.
3. My brother plays baseball every summer.

F. Write the paragraph so that it is a present-tense paragraph.

The flowers were starting to grow. The birds were singing. The grass was turning green. Summer was coming.

STOP END OF LESSON 98.

A. Read the description.

The tree has a broken branch. It is a big tree. A bird is in the tree.

Instructions:

Write the number of the tree the description is about.

1   2   3

B. Write a story about the picture. Tell what happened just before the picture. Tell what happened in the picture. Tell what the people said. Tell what happened next. Write all the sentences in the past tense.

| cake | batter | spilled | mess | oven |

Independent Work

C. Write each sentence with a contraction in place of the underlined words.

1. You <u>should not</u> say that.
2. <u>She is</u> still sleeping.
3. <u>You will</u> like this story.

D. Write one sentence with each simple subject.

1. father
2. pencils
3. water
4. Jane

E. Write the paragraph so that it is a present-tense paragraph.

It was dark and cool in the barn. The cows were mooing. The sun was about to rise. The day was beginning.

STOP END OF LESSON 99.

A. Read the description.

The tree has a broken branch. A bird is in the tree. It is a small tree.

Instructions:

1. Write the number of the tree the description is about.
2. Write a description of tree 1.

1   2   3   4

B. Write a story about the picture. Tell what happened just before the picture. Tell what happened in the picture. Tell what the people said. Tell what happened next. Write all the sentences in the past tense.

Maria

Nelson

| frightened | movie | scary |

Independent Work

C. Complete each analogy.

1. Cutting is to a knife as painting is to a ⬜.
2. A bottle is to glass as a tire is to ⬜.
3. A school is to learning as a bedroom is to ⬜.
4. Thin is to thick as light is to ⬜.

D. Write each statement another way by moving words that are in the predicate.

1. When it rains, the river gets muddy.
2. There is a piece of cake in the refrigerator.

E. Write the paragraph so that it is a present-tense paragraph.

     Nora liked to eat oranges. She ate lots and lots of oranges. Nora was very healthy.

STOP END OF LESSON 100.

A. Read the description.

The man is wearing glasses. He is bald. He is wearing a shirt.

1   2   3   4

Read the instructions.

1. Write the number of the man the description is about.
2. Write a description of man number 1.

B. Write five comparisons of house A and house B.

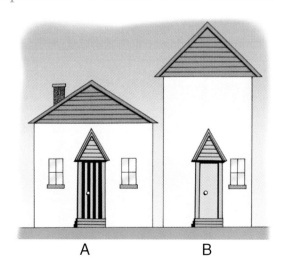

A   B

striped
wider
house
plain
chimney
narrower
windows

Independent Work

C. Follow the directions.

1. First draw a triangle.
2. Then write the number **9** below the triangle.
3. Then draw a big circle around the number **9** and the triangle.
4. Then write the letter **X** inside the triangle.

D. Write the paragraph so that it is a past-tense paragraph.

      The cage door is standing open. The monkey is coming out of its cage. People are running away. Everyone is shouting and laughing.

E. Write one sentence with each simple subject.

1. ball
2. snake
3. dishes
4. they

F. Write one sentence with each verb.

1. flew
2. is building
3. can smell
4. jumped

STOP END OF LESSON 101.

A. Read the description.

The man is wearing glasses. He does not have a beard. He is not wearing a shirt.

1   2   3   4

Read the instructions.

1. Write the number of the man the description is about.
2. Write a description of man number 2.

B. Write four comparisons of bike A and bike B.

| flat tire | hand brakes |

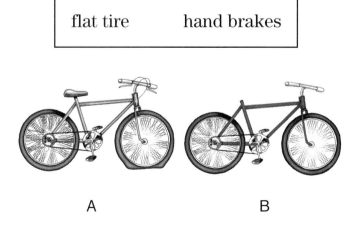

A   B

Independent Work

C. Write each sentence **without** using a contraction.

1. I've fished in that river.
2. The boys didn't see the car.
3. We couldn't go to the circus.

D. Write one sentence with each simple subject.

1. shovel
2. flowers
3. John
4. milk

E. Write each sentence another way by moving words that are in the predicate.

1. Under the bed, there was an old shoe.
2. The pool will open at two o'clock.
3. He eats a big breakfast every morning.

F. Write the paragraph so that it is a past-tense paragraph.

There is a big hole in Tom's boat. Water is running in through the hole. The boat is sinking. Tom is shouting, "Help!"

STOP END OF LESSON 102.

A. Write the statements.

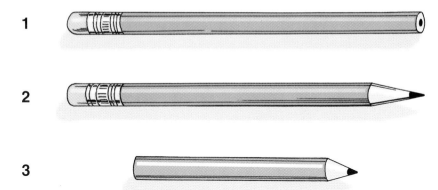

1. Write a **true** statement about the third pencil.
2. Write a **false** statement about the third pencil.
3. Write a **maybe** statement about the third pencil.

B. Write five comparisons of twin A and twin B.

twin	sleeved	sandals	glasses	shirt

A   B

Independent Work

C. Write one sentence with each simple subject.

1. you   3. it
2. worms   4. he

D. Write the paragraph so that it is a present-tense paragraph.

      The lightning was flashing. The wind was blowing. The rain was coming down hard. Jim and Sue were running for the house.

E. Follow the directions.

1. First write the number **4.**
2. Then write the number **8** above the number **4.**
3. Then draw a horizontal line between the two numbers.
4. Then write the letter **O** above one end of the horizontal line.

F. Write each sentence with a contraction in place of the underlined words.

1. They <u>did not</u> set the table.
2. <u>I am</u> starting the fire.
3. <u>You are</u> spilling the paint.

STOP END OF LESSON 103.

A. Write the statements.

1. Write a **false** statement about the second wagon.
2. Write a **true** statement about the second wagon.
3. Write a **maybe** statement about the second wagon.
4. Write a **true** statement about the first wagon.

B. Write five comparisons of tree A and tree B.

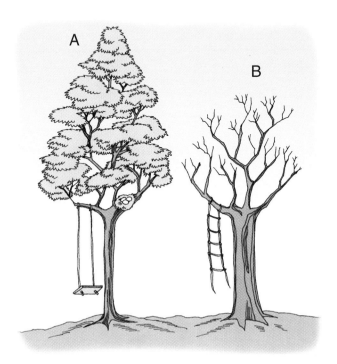

trunk
leaves
narrower
ladder
swing

Independent Work

C. Write each sentence another way by moving words that are in the predicate.

1. Before you leave, talk to the teacher.
2. Every evening, we watch the sun set.
3. The air smelled fresh after the rain.

D. Write one sentence with each verb.

1. were pushing
2. listened
3. will make
4. is

E. Write the paragraph so that it is a past-tense paragraph.

Inez is hot and tired. She is sitting in the shade of a tree. She is drinking a bottle of cold juice. A fly is buzzing around her head.

F. Write the abbreviation for each word.

1. Mister
2. yard
3. mile
4. inch
5. Street
6. hour
7. Doctor
8. foot

STOP END OF LESSON 104.

A. Write the statements.

1. Write a **false** statement about the first bicycle.
2. Write a **true** statement about the first bicycle.
3. Write a **maybe** statement about the first bicycle.
4. Write a **true** statement about the third bicycle.
5. Write a **false** statement about the third bicycle.
6. Write a **maybe** statement about the third bicycle.

B.   Zirk is a robot who does only what you tell him to do. If you want him to do something, you have to give him clear instructions in writing. Then he reads your instructions and does exactly what you tell him to do.

Here are the first three instructions to Zirk for fixing a bowl of cereal.

- Put a box of cereal on the kitchen table.
- Put a cereal bowl on the kitchen table.
- Put a carton of milk on the kitchen table.

Write at least three more instructions to Zirk for fixing a bowl of cereal.

pour	cereal	milk	spoon

Independent Work

C. Read the description.

The kite has a short tail. It is a big kite. It is covered with stripes.

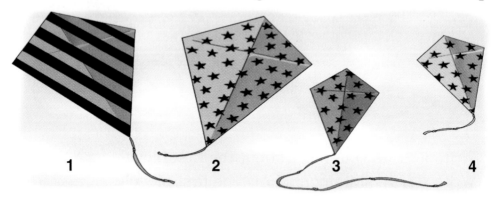

Read the instructions.

1. Write the number of the kite the description is about.
2. Write a description of kite number 4.

D. Complete each analogy.

1. A ball is to toys as a tree is to _____ .
2. A fish is to swimming as a bird is to _____ .
3. A barn is to a cow as a zoo is to a _____ .
4. Glad is to happy as narrow is to _____ .
5. A cherry is to red as milk is to _____ .

E. Write one sentence with each verb.

1. will paint   3. was
2. is   4. were chasing

 **STOP** END OF LESSON 105.

212

A.   If you want Zirk the robot to do something, you have to give him clear instructions in writing. He reads your instructions and does exactly what you tell him to do.

    Here are the first four instructions to Zirk for making buttered toast.

- Put one slice of bread in the toaster.
- Toast the bread until it's done.
- Put the toasted bread on the kitchen counter.
- Put a stick of butter on the kitchen counter.

Write at least three more instructions to Zirk so he can finish making the buttered toast.

knife	kitchen counter	cut
butter	toast	spread

Independent Work

B. Write one sentence with each simple subject.

1. game
2. marbles
3. airplane
4. she

C. Read the description.

     A tree is next to the house. The house has a chimney. Two windows in the front of the house are broken.

1   2   3   4

Read the instructions.

1. Write the number of the house the description is about.
2. Write a description of house number 3.

D. Write the statements.

1   2   3

1. Write a **maybe** statement about the first umbrella.
2. Write a **true** statement about the first umbrella.
3. Write a **false** statement about the first umbrella.
4. Write a **true** statement about the third umbrella.
5. Write a **false** statement about the third umbrella.
6. Write a **maybe** statement about the third umbrella.

 END OF LESSON 106.

214

A.   Zirk the robot is still working in the kitchen. Here are the first three instructions to Zirk for making orange juice.

- Put a can of frozen orange juice on the kitchen counter.
- Put an empty pitcher on the kitchen counter.
- Put a long spoon on the kitchen counter.

Write at least four instructions to Zirk so he can finish making the orange juice.

| open | frozen orange juice | | water |
| pitcher | pour | spoon | stir |

Independent Work

B. Follow the directions.

1. First draw a rectangle.
2. Then draw a vertical line through the middle of the rectangle.
3. Then write the letter **R** in the right half of the rectangle.
4. Then write the letter **L** in the left half of the rectangle.
5. Then draw a big triangle around the rectangle.

C. Write the paragraph so that it is a present-tense paragraph.

The spider was huge. It was black with a bright orange spot on its back. The spider was making a beautiful web in the bushes.

D. Read the description.

The girl is smiling. She has short hair. She is not wearing glasses.

1   2   3   4

Read the instructions.

1. Write the number of the girl the description is about.
2. Write a description of girl number 4.

E. Write one sentence with each simple subject.

1. monkey   3. toys
2. boat   4. Bill

STOP END OF LESSON 107.

A. Write the descriptions.

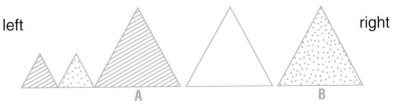

left   right

A   B

1. Write a description telling **where** figure A is.
2. Write a description telling **how** figure A **looks.**
3. Write a description telling **where** figure B is.
4. Write a description telling **how** figure B **looks.**

B. Picture B is different from picture A in five ways. Write five instructions to Zirk the robot for making picture B look like picture A.

| house |
| path |
| cloud |
| floor |
| yard |

A   B

Independent Work

C. Write one sentence with each verb.

1. will cry
2. was smiling
3. kicked
4. is stirring

D. Write the statements.

1   2   3

1. Write a **maybe** statement about the first wagon.
2. Write a **true** statement about the first wagon.
3. Write a **false** statement about the first wagon.
4. Write a **false** statement about the third wagon.
5. Write a **true** statement about the third wagon.
6. Write a **maybe** statement about the third wagon.

E. Complete each analogy.

1. A car is to metal as a bottle is to _____ .
2. An eraser is to a pencil as a page is to a _____ .
3. A house is to people as a barn is to _____ .
4. A pen is to writing as a saw is to _____ .
5. Above is to below as wet is to _____ .

F. Write each sentence **without** using a contraction.

1. The turtle isn't going anywhere.
2. Jill couldn't find her glasses.
3. They'll feed the monkeys.

STOP END OF LESSON 108.

A. Write the descriptions.

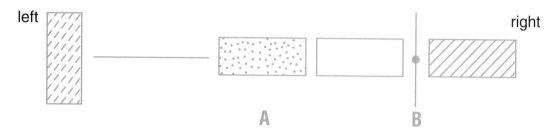

left
right

A
B

1. Write a description telling **where** figure A is.
2. Write a description telling **how** figure A **looks.**
3. Write a description telling **where** figure B is.
4. Write a description telling **how** figure B **looks.**

B. Menu B is different from menu A in six ways. Write six instructions to Zirk the robot for making menu B look like menu A.

Menu A

Breakfast Nook	
1. Steak and Eggs	$6.00
2. Bacon and Eggs	$5.00
3. Nothing but Eggs	$4.00
4. Fruit Salad	$3.00
5. Bowl of Cereal	$2.00
6. Toast and Jam	$1.00

Menu B

Breakfast Nook	
1. Steak and Eggs	$5.00
2. Ham and Eggs	$5.00
3. Nothing	$4.00
4. Fruit and Salad	$3.00
5. Bowl of Cereal	$1.00
6. Toasted Jam	$1.00

Independent Work

There were no clouds in the sky. The sun was hot. Under the trees, the boys were swimming in the pond. The water was cool and fresh. It was a beautiful afternoon.

1. First draw a horizontal line.
2. Then write the word **zoo** above the horizontal line.
3. Then draw another horizontal line above the word **zoo.**
4. Then draw a vertical line to the right of the word **zoo.**
5. Then draw another vertical line to the left of the word **zoo.**

The kite has stars on it. It has a long tail. It is a small kite.

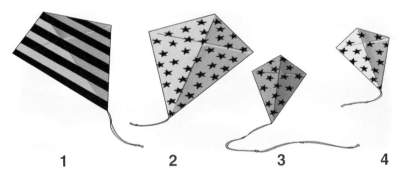

1   2   3   4

1. Write the number of the kite the description is about.
2. Write a description of kite number 2.

1. nail   3. mother
2. trees   4. dirt

STOP END OF LESSON 109.

A. Write the descriptions.

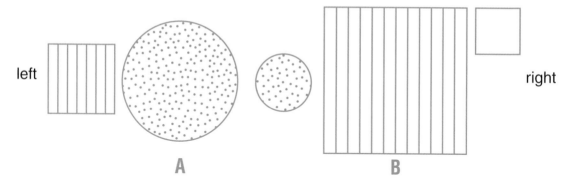

left A B right

1. Write a description telling **where** figure A is.
2. Write a description telling **how** figure A **looks.**
3. Write a description telling **where** figure B is.
4. Write a description telling **how** figure B **looks.**

B.   Zirk is still working in the kitchen. Here are the first two instructions to Zirk for making a peanut-butter-and-jelly sandwich.

- Put two pieces of bread on the kitchen counter.
- Put a jar of peanut butter on the kitchen counter.

Write at least four instructions to Zirk so he can finish making the peanut-butter-and-jelly sandwich.

jar	jelly	peanut butter
kitchen counter	knife	spread

Independent Work

C. Read the description.

> The girl is wearing glasses. Her hair is long. She is not smiling.

1   2   3   4

Read the instructions.

1. Write the number of the girl the description is about.
2. Write a description of girl number 2.

D. Write one sentence with each simple subject.

   1. window   2. men   3. dog   4. bug

E. Write the statements.

1. Write a **true** statement about the second shirt.
2. Write a **false** statement about the second shirt.
3. Write a **maybe** statement about the second shirt.
4. Write a **false** statement about the third shirt.
5. Write a **true** statement about the third shirt.

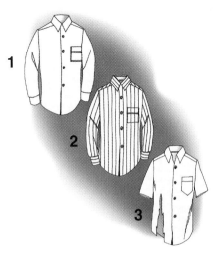

STOP END OF LESSON 110.

A. The dishwasher is broken, so Zirk has to wash the dishes by hand. Here are the first two instructions to Zirk for washing the dishes by hand.

- Put the dirty dishes in the kitchen sink.
- Fill the sink with hot water.

Write at least four more instructions to Zirk so he can finish washing the dishes by hand.

detergent	sponge	rinse	drying rack

Independent Work

B. Read the description.

The house has two broken windows in the front. The house has a chimney. There are no trees near the house.

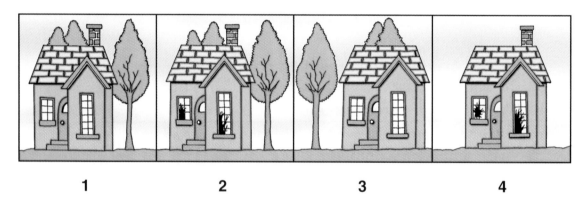

1   2   3   4

Read the instructions.

1. Write the number of the house the description is about.
2. Write a description of house number 1.

C. Follow the directions.

1. First draw a rectangle.
2. Then draw a vertical line through the middle of the rectangle.
3. Then write the number **8** in the left side of the rectangle.
4. Then write the number **9** in the right side of the rectangle.
5. Then draw a circle around the number **8.**

D. Write the descriptions.

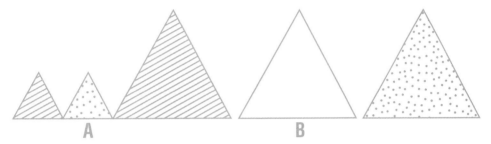

1. Write a description telling **where** figure A is.
2. Write a description telling **how** figure A **looks.**
3. Write a description telling **where** figure B is.
4. Write a description telling **how** figure B **looks.**

STOP END OF LESSON 111.

A. Menu B is different from menu A in five ways. Write five instructions to Zirk the robot for making menu B look like menu A.

price	change	dish	name

Menu A	**Menu B**

Lunch and Munch

	Menu A			Menu B	
1.	Ham Sandwich	5 dollars	1.	Sam Handwich	5 dollars
2.	Cheeseburger	4 dollars	2.	Cheeseburger	4 dollars
3.	Hamburger	3 dollars	3.	Hamburger	4 dollars
4.	Fruit Salad	3 dollars	4.	Fruit Salad	3 dollars
5.	Cheese Sandwich	3 dollars	5.	Choose Sandwich	3 dollars
6.	Milkshake	2 dollars	6.	Milkquake	2 dollars
7.	Dessert	2 dollars	7.	Desert	2 dollars

Independent Work

B. Write the descriptions.

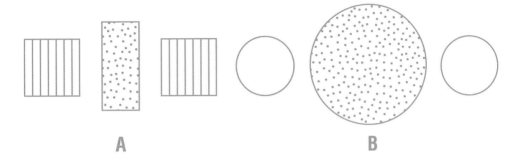

A

B

1. Write a description telling **where** figure A is.
2. Write a description telling **how** figure A **looks.**
3. Write a description telling **where** figure B is.
4. Write a description telling **how** figure B **looks.**

C. Follow the directions.

1. First write the number **9.**
2. Then write the number **8** to the right of the number **9.**
3. Then write the number **7** under the number **8.**
4. Then draw a line from the number **9** to the number **8.**
5. Then draw a line from the number **8** to the number **7.**

D. Write the paragraph in the past tense.

Devin is a happy boy. His father is taking him to camp. Devin likes camp a lot.

STOP END OF LESSON 112.

A.   Zirk needs to sweep crumbs off the kitchen floor. Here is the first instruction to Zirk for sweeping up the crumbs.

- Take the broom and dustpan out of the kitchen closet.

Write at least four more instructions to Zirk so he can sweep up the crumbs.

sweep	pile	dustpan	wastebasket	closet

Independent Work

B. Write the descriptions.

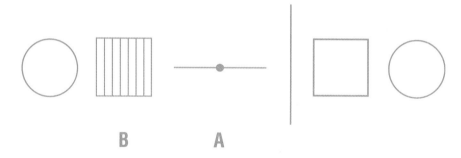

B   A

1. Write a description telling **where** figure A is.
2. Write a description telling **how** figure A **looks.**
3. Write a description telling **where** figure B is.
4. Write a description telling **how** figure B **looks.**

C. Follow the directions.

1. First draw a triangle.
2. Then write the number **5** inside the triangle.
3. Then write the word **water** to the right of the triangle.
4. Then draw a vertical line between the triangle and the word **water.**

STOP END OF LESSON 113.

A. Copy the sentence on your paper. Then complete the story. Write at least three paragraphs.

> Tom's sister's birthday is tomorrow, but Tom doesn't have any money for her present.

Independent Work

B. Write the descriptions.

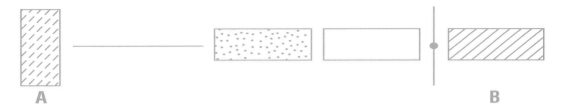

1. Write a description telling **where** figure A is.
2. Write a description telling **how** figure A **looks.**
3. Write a description telling **where** figure B is.
4. Write a description telling **how** figure B **looks.**

C. Follow the directions.

1. First write the number **4.**
2. Then draw a circle to the left of the number **4.**
3. Then draw a rectangle to the right of the number **4.**
4. Then draw a triangle above the number **4.**
5. Then draw a horizontal line under the number **4.**

D. Write each sentence **without** using a contraction.

1. He'll fix the bathtub.
2. The worms weren't in the can.
3. His parents didn't drive him to school.

STOP END OF LESSON 114.

A. Copy the sentence on your paper. Then complete the story. Write at least three paragraphs.

> Mira wanted to play on the soccer team, but she couldn't run very fast.

Independent Work

B. Write the descriptions.

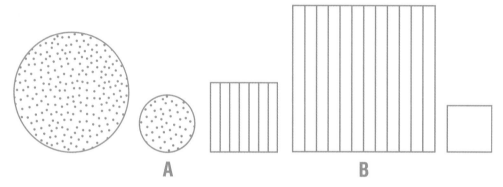

1. Write a description telling **where** figure A is.
2. Write a description telling **how** figure A **looks.**
3. Write a description telling **where** figure B is.
4. Write a description telling **how** figure B **looks.**

C. Follow the directions.

1. First draw a circle.
2. Then write the number **8** in the middle of the circle.
3. Then draw a rectangle around the circle.
4. Then draw a horizontal line below the rectangle.

D. Write the paragraph in the past tense.

> Reba and Jeff are digging in the garden. They are digging up worms. They are going fishing in the pond.

 END OF LESSON 115.

A. Copy the sentences on your paper. Then complete the story. Write at least three paragraphs.

> A sudden, loud boom woke everybody in the house. Then they saw strange lights outside the windows.

Independent Work

B. Write the descriptions.

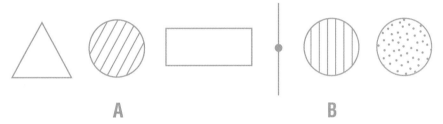

A   B

1. Write a description telling **where** figure A is.
2. Write a description telling **how** figure A **looks.**
3. Write a description telling **where** figure B is.
4. Write a description telling **how** figure B **looks.**

C. Follow the directions.

1. First write the number **1.**
2. Then write the number **2** below the number **1.**
3. Then write the number **3** below the number **2.**
4. Then draw a horizontal line between the number **1** and the number **2.**

D. Write each sentence with a contraction in place of the underlined words.

1. <u>They have</u> seen everything.
2. The game <u>is not</u> over yet.
3. <u>He will</u> put away the toys.

STOP END OF LESSON 116.

A. Copy the sentences on your paper. Then complete the story. Write at least three paragraphs.

> "Get into the lifeboats," shouted the captain. "We're starting to sink."

Independent Work

B. Write the descriptions.

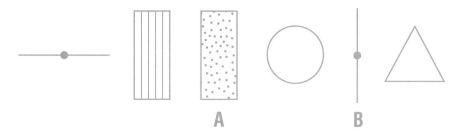

1. Write a description telling **where** figure A is.
2. Write a description telling **how** figure A **looks.**
3. Write a description telling **where** figure B is.
4. Write a description telling **how** figure B **looks.**

C. Follow the directions.

1. First draw a vertical line.
2. Then write the word **yes** on the left side of the vertical line.
3. Then write the word **no** on the right side of the vertical line.
4. Then draw a circle around the word **yes.**
5. Then draw a rectangle around the word **no.**

D. Read the description.

The elephant's trunk is hanging down. A monkey is sitting on the elephant's head. The elephant is small.

Read the instructions.

1. Write the number of the elephant the description is about.
2. Write a description of elephant number 3.

 END OF LESSON 117.

A.   Zirk needs to wash his hands in the kitchen sink. A bar of soap and a hand towel are already next to the sink. The bar of soap is in a soap dish. Here are the first two instructions to Zirk for washing and drying his hands.

- Turn on the warm water in the sink.
- Put your hands in the warm water for a few seconds.

Write at least three more instructions to Zirk so he can finish washing and drying his hands.

bar of soap	rub	soap dish	rinse
	turn off	dry	towel

Independent Work

B. Write each sentence **without** using a contraction.

1. She couldn't open the door.
2. He'll have to stay after school.
3. I'm tired of playing.

C. Follow the directions.

1. First draw a horizontal line.
2. Then draw another horizontal line above the first horizontal line.
3. Then draw a line from the left end of one horizontal line to the left end of the other horizontal line.
4. Then draw a line from the right end of the one horizontal line to the right end of the other horizontal line.

D. Write the paragraph in the past tense.

Jill is trying to climb the big tree. She is halfway up. The bark is scratching her arms. She is getting tired, but she is not stopping.

 **STOP** END OF LESSON 118.

A. Write five comparisons of desk A and desk B.

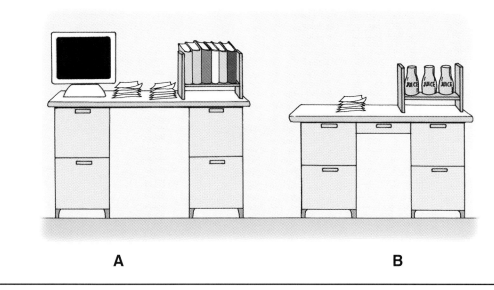

A   B

drawers	paper	bigger	desk	computer	shelf	bottles

Independent Work

B. Write each present-tense statement as a past-tense statement. Write each past-tense statement as a present-tense statement.

1. The mouse was eating cheese.
2. The eggs were too old.
3. His hat is hanging in the closet.
4. Fred runs to school every morning.
5. Juanita ties her shoes tightly.

C. Write each sentence with a contraction in place of the underlined words.

1. The pie <u>was not</u> big enough.
2. <u>We have</u> picked all the oranges.
3. I <u>should not</u> talk so much.

D. Read the description.

The elephant is big. His trunk is curled up. A bird is sitting on the elephant's head.

Read the instructions.

1. Write the number of the elephant the description is about.
2. Write a description of elephant number 4.

 END OF LESSON 119.

A. Copy the sentence on your paper. Then complete the story. Write at least three paragraphs.

> Sally didn't know it yet, but today would be the most important day of her life.

Independent Work

B. Follow the directions.

1. First draw a vertical line.
2. Then write the word **wet** on the left side of the line.
3. Then write the word **dry** on the right side of the line.
4. Then draw a circle around the word **wet.**
5. Then draw a triangle around the word **dry.**

C. Write each sentence with a contraction in place of the underlined words.

1. Those people <u>are not</u> going with us.
2. <u>You have</u> eaten all the sandwiches.
3. Diego <u>should not</u> stay out late.

D. Write each sentence **without** using a contraction.

1. The sun didn't come out today.
2. The tiger couldn't get out of the cage.
3. You're doing a good job.

STOP END OF LESSON 120.

A. Read the table.

	un	**at**	**it**
s	sun	sat	sit
f	fun	fat	fit
b	bun	bat	bit

B. Write three jokes.

1. | wheels   garbage truck   flies |

2. | south   birds   winter |

3. | outside   chicken   feathers |

C. Copy the sentences. Then complete the story. Write at least three paragraphs.

    The forest was dark, quiet and still. Suddenly, a low, rumbling noise shook the trees and woke up the birds.

GO TO PAGE 221 IN YOUR WORKBOOK.

A. Read the table.

	6	**7**	**8**	**9**
1	16	17	18	19
2	26	27	28	29
3	36	37	38	39
4	46	47	48	49

B. Write three jokes.

1. | zebra   sunburned |

2. | watchdog   because |

3. | remember   bees   words   hum |

C.   Zirk the robot is trying to make bedroom B look just like bedroom A. Write five instructions to Zirk that explain how to make bedroom B match bedroom A.

curtains	windows	chair	corner
round	picture	square	lamp

A

B

GO TO PAGE 222 IN YOUR WORKBOOK.

A. Read the table.

	how many fly	**how many lay eggs**
insects	some	all
mammals	some	some
birds	some	all
fish	some	some

B. Write three jokes.

1. | time   elephant   chair |

2. | skunk   smelling |

3. | slippers   pair   bananas |

C.   Here are the first two instructions to Zirk for washing and drying your laundry.

- Put a cup of laundry soap in the washing machine.
- Put the dirty clothes in the washing machine.

Write at least three more instructions to Zirk so he can finish washing and drying your laundry.

| start   washing machine   stops   dryer |

GO TO PAGE 223 IN YOUR WORKBOOK.

A. Compare this joke to what you wrote.

Bill worked for a shipping company. His boss said, "Please take these penguins to the zoo."

A few hours later, the boss saw Bill walking along the street with the penguins. The boss said, "I told you to take those penguins to the zoo."

Bill said, "I did. We had such a good time that now we're going to the movies."

B. Write five comparisons of dog A and dog B.

taller	pointy	floppy	thinner	plain

A   B

STOP END OF LESSON 124.

A. Compare this joke to what you wrote.

One day a tall man started growing shorter. His clothes didn't fit, and his shoes were too big.

The man went to the doctor and said, "I keep getting shorter. What should I do?"

The doctor said, "You'll just have to be a little patient."

B. Copy the sentences. Then complete the story. Write at least three paragraphs.

From far away, the planet Zanza looked like a bright yellow ball. The people on the spaceship thought it would be a good place to land.

STOP END OF LESSON 125.

LESSON 126

A. Compare this joke to what you wrote.

A sign outside the shoe store said, "Beware of the dog." But when Jane went into the store, all she saw was a big dog sleeping on the floor.

One day, Jane asked the owner, "Why does your sign say to beware of the dog?"

The owner answered, "Because people kept tripping over him."

B. Zirk needs to change a lightbulb in a table lamp. He has to be careful with this job because electricity is dangerous. Here are the first two instructions to Zirk for changing the lightbulb.

- Unplug the table lamp.
- Unscrew the old lightbulb.

Write at least three more instructions to Zirk so he can finish changing the lightbulb.

new bulb	plug in	turn on
throw away	screw in	

STOP END OF LESSON 126.

A. Compare this story to what you wrote.

A rabbit and a turtle had a race. Everybody thought the rabbit would win because it was much faster than the turtle. The rabbit got so far ahead that it took a nap.

While the rabbit was napping, the turtle passed it and won the race.

This story shows that if you are slow and steady, you will win the race.

B. Phone list B is different from phone list A in five ways. Write five instructions to Zirk the robot for making phone list B look like phone list A.

A
Get Well Hospital Phone List
1. Emergency Room 525-2525
2. Front Desk 525-5252
3. Kids' Doctor 525-1234
4. Operating Room 525-9876
5. Billing 525-9999
6. Adults' Doctor 525-5555
7. Nurses' Station 525-2468

B
Get Well Hospital Phone List
1. Emergency Room 525-2424
2. Back Desk 525-5252
3. Kids' Doctor 525-1234
4. Operating Office 525-9876
5. Building 525-9999
6. Adults' Doctor 525-5555
7. Nurses' Station 555-2468

STOP END OF LESSON 127.

245

A. Compare this story to what you wrote.

A hungry fox saw a bunch of grapes hanging from a high tree branch.

The fox said, "I'd like to eat those grapes." So he jumped high in the air, again and again, but he couldn't reach them. At last he gave up and said, "I'm sure those grapes are sour."

This story shows that it is easy to dislike what you cannot get.

B. Copy the sentences. Then complete the story. Write at least three paragraphs.

Homer woke up one morning and discovered he was all alone in the house. His parents were gone, and so were his brother and sister.

STOP END OF LESSON 128.

A. Compare this story to what you wrote.

A thirsty crow found a pitcher that had just a little bit of water at the bottom. The crow couldn't reach the water.

Then the crow had an idea. She found a pebble and dropped it into the pitcher. The water rose a little bit. So the crow dropped pebbles into the water until the water rose to the top of the pitcher. Then she drank the water.

This story shows that when you need something, you get good ideas.

B. Listen to these paragraphs.

Frida is shopping in a store that's about to close for the day. She picks out a flashlight and a hat and takes them to the checkout counter. Suddenly, she discovers she doesn't have enough money to pay for both things. Frida can buy either the flashlight or the hat, but not both.

Because the store is closing, Frida doesn't have enough time to walk home and get more money. She can come back to the store tomorrow, but she'd really like to buy something today.

What do you think Frida should do? Write two paragraphs to explain your answer.

- In the first paragraph, tell what you think Frida should do. Start with the words **I think Frida should.**

- In the second paragraph, explain why your choice is a good one. Start with the words **This is a good choice because.**

today	flashlight	tomorrow

STOP END OF LESSON 129.

A. Compare this passage to what you wrote.

Mercury is close to the sun, so it doesn't have to go very far when it orbits the sun. Mars is farther from the sun. It has to travel farther when it orbits the sun. So Mars takes longer to orbit the sun than Mercury does.

B. Listen to these paragraphs.

Ahmed's basketball team is losing a game by one point, with just a few seconds left to play. Ahmed is dribbling the ball far away from the basket. If he makes a basket from there, his team will score two points, and they will win the game. But it's a hard shot.

Suddenly, Ahmed sees his teammate Isaac standing close to the basket. If Ahmed passes the ball, Isaac will have an easy shot at the basket. But time is running out.

What do you think Ahmed should do? Write two paragraphs to explain your answer.

- In the first paragraph, tell what you think Ahmed should do. Start with the words **I think Ahmed should.**

- In the second paragraph, explain why your choice is a good one. Start with the words **This is a good choice because.**

STOP END OF LESSON 130.

A. Compare this passage to the one you wrote.

What makes birds different from other animals? Birds can lay eggs, but so can many other animals, such as fish and frogs. So, laying eggs doesn't make birds different.

Birds are the only animals that are covered with feathers. So, feathers make birds different.

B. Listen to these paragraphs.

Elvira has been saving money all year to buy a bicycle. She visits the bike store and looks at two different bikes. The first is a single-speed bike. The bike is cheap, but it is hard to pedal up hills.

The second bike has seven speeds. It costs all the money Elvira has, but it is easy to pedal up hills. Elvira's town has both hilly parts and flat parts.

What do you think Elvira should do? Write two paragraphs to explain your answer.

- In the first paragraph, tell what you think Elvira should do. Start with the words **I think Elvira should.**
- In the second paragraph, explain why your choice is a good one. Start with the words **This is a good choice because.**

Independent Work

C. Compare this paragraph to the one you corrected in part A of your workbook. The corrections are in **red type.**

Sandra **has** two cats. **One** cat is named Binky, and the other **is** named Slinky. **Binky** and Slinky are always playing together. Binky always **chases** Slinky. Then they wrestle on the rug. Binky and Slinky **are** not the same size. Binky is bigger, but **Slinky is** faster. **Sandra loves** both her cats very much. They love her too.

D. Compare this paragraph to the one you corrected in part C of your workbook. The corrections are in **red type.**

Kareem **lives** in a big city. **He** goes to a big school, and he **plays** in a big park. Everything around Kareem is big. **The** buildings **are** big, the cars are big and the streets **are** big. But **Kareem** is not big. **He's** just a little boy.

STOP END OF LESSON 131.

A. Listen to these paragraphs.

Manny wakes up early one morning and walks into the kitchen. He almost always eats a bowl of cereal before school, but today he has more time to eat breakfast.

Manny looks in the refrigerator and sees some bacon and eggs. They look good, but Manny isn't quite sure how to cook them. He also doesn't like cleaning pans after he cooks. Still, the bacon and eggs look a lot better than the same old cereal.

What do you think Manny should eat for breakfast? Write two paragraphs to explain your answer.

- In the first paragraph, tell what you think Manny should eat for breakfast. Start with the words **I think Manny should.**
- In the second paragraph, explain why your choice is a good one. Start with the words **This is a good choice because.**

B. Zirk has to put on a pair of shoes with shoelaces so he can go outside. He already has socks on his feet. Here are the first two instructions to Zirk for putting on his shoes with shoelaces.

- Put your shoes on the floor.
- Put your right foot into the right shoe.

Write at least three more instructions to Zirk so he can finish putting on the shoes. Try to use some of the words in the box.

tighten	shoelaces	tie	bow

Independent Work

C. Compare this paragraph to the one you corrected in part A of your workbook. The corrections are in **red type**.

We had a big storm last night. The rain fell, the thunder **boomed** and the lightning **flashed**. **Many** people and animals **got** wet. We left the windows down on our car, so the car seats **got** wet too. We couldn't **sit** down in the car until the seats dried. **What** a mess.

D. Compare this paragraph to the one you corrected in part B of your workbook. The corrections are in **red type**.

Riding a bike is fun, but it can be dangerous. If you **fall** off a bike, you can **hurt** your head. **That's** why you should always **wear** a helmet when you ride a bike. When you **ride** on a street, you should always **stay** in a bike lane or far to the side. Never ride in the middle of the street where cars can **hit** you.

STOP END OF LESSON 132.

Independent Work

A. Compare this story to the one you wrote in part C of your workbook.

> One day, a big lion caught a little mouse. The mouse begged, "If you let me go, I will save your life."
>
> The lion laughed to think that a mouse could save his life. But he was a kind lion, so he let the mouse go.
>
> The next day, a hunter trapped the lion and tied him up with rope. The mouse ran up to the lion and chewed through the rope.
>
> The lion said to the mouse, "You saved my life."
>
> This story shows that kindness is never wasted.

B. Compare this paragraph to the one you corrected in part B of your workbook. The corrections are in **red type.**

> Tomorrow, Frank will be **working** around the house. **First** he will make his bed. **Then** he will **take** out the trash. After that, he will **pull** weeds out of the yard. When Frank is all done with these jobs, he will **take** a nap. **All** that hard work will **make** him tired.

STOP END OF LESSON 133.

Independent Work

A. Compare this passage to what you wrote in part C of your workbook.

There are two main kinds of animals. One kind has a backbone. Dogs, frogs, chickens, sharks and snakes have backbones. Bees, spiders, worms, snails and ants do not have backbones.

People are animals with backbones. That hard thing in the middle of your back is your backbone.

B. Compare this joke to the one you corrected in part B of your workbook. The corrections are in **red type.**

Harold went to a restaurant and looked at the menu. He couldn't decide if he **wanted** peach pie, apple pie or cherry pie. **After** he **thought** for a long time, he ordered apple pie.

When Harold got the pie, he took a big bite**. He** called the waiter over and **said,** "This apple pie tastes like glue."

"That's funny," the waiter said. "The apple pie is not supposed to taste like glue. **The** cherry pie and the peach pie are supposed to taste like glue."

STOP END OF LESSON 134.

254

A. Listen to these paragraphs.

The Garcia family drives to a theater at seven o'clock to see a movie called *The Golden Parrot.* When they get to the theater, the seven o'clock show is sold out, but there are still tickets for the nine o'clock show. The theater also has tickets for a seven o'clock movie called *Hearts and Flowers.*

Mr. and Mrs. Garcia want to see *Hearts and Flowers*, but their two children want to wait for the nine o'clock showing of *The Golden Parrot.* Mr. Garcia says two hours is too long to wait.

What do you think the Garcias should do? Write two paragraphs to explain your answer.

- In the first paragraph, tell what you think the Garcias should do. Start with the words **I think the Garcias should.**
- In the second paragraph, explain why your choice is a good one. Start with the words **This is a good choice because.**

Independent Work

B. Compare this joke to the one you corrected in part B of your workbook. The corrections are in **red type.**

After Harold ate at the restaurant with the bad pies, he went to another restaurant. He **said** to himself, "**I'm** tired of eating pies that taste like glue. Maybe I'll try some soup instead.**"**

Harold **ordered** tomato soup. When the waiter came with the soup, Harold looked in the bowl and **saw** a fly. "What is this fly doing in my soup**?"** Harold asked.

The waiter said**,** "I'm pretty sure **he's** swimming."

C. Compare this paragraph to the one you corrected in part C of your workbook. The corrections are in **red type.**

Here's how Tom and Linda write reports. They **think** about what they **want** to write. Then they make an outline. They write the report, but they know that they need to **make** some changes. So one of them **reads** what they **wrote**, and the other one listens. They hear those **parts** that don't sound right. They fix up all **mistakes**. Then they read it again. The last thing they do is look at each **sentence** very **carefully** and change anything that is wrong. Tom and Linda **write** some very good **reports**.

STOP END OF LESSON 135.

A. Use the table and the outline to write the second paragraph.

	orbit time	**distance from the sun**	**number of moons**
Mercury	88 days	36 million miles	none
Venus	225 days	67 million miles	none
Earth	365 days	93 million miles	one
Mars	687 days	142 million miles	two
Jupiter	about 12 years	484 million miles	at least 60
Saturn	about 30 years	887 million miles	at least 30

1. Three ways Mercury is different from Earth
   a. Mercury has a shorter orbit time.
   b. Mercury is closer to the sun.
   c. Mercury has no moons.

     Mercury is different from Earth in several ways. To begin with, Mercury has a much shorter orbit time than Earth. Mercury orbits the sun in just 88 days, but Earth orbits the sun in 365 days. Also, Mercury is much closer to the sun. It's only 36 million miles from the sun, but Earth is 93 million miles from the sun. Finally, Mercury doesn't have a moon. Earth does have a moon.

2. Three ways Mars is different from Earth
   a. Mars has a longer orbit time.
   b. Mars is farther from the sun.
   c. Mars has more moons.

B. Listen to these paragraphs.

Sanjay feels out of shape. His doctor says he needs more exercise, like running or walking. She tells Sanjay to join a health club and use the walking machines. But the health club costs a lot of money.

The doctor says Sanjay could also get exercise by walking to work. Sanjay knows that it will take at least an hour to walk to work. That means he will have to get up an hour earlier every morning. He's not happy about that idea because an hour seems like too much time to spend walking. He's also not happy with the idea of spending so much money for the health club.

What do you think Sanjay should do? Write two paragraphs to explain your answer.

• In the first paragraph, tell what you think Sanjay should do. Start with the words **I think Sanjay should.**

• In the second paragraph, explain why your choice is a good one. Start with the words **This is a good choice because.**

Independent Work

C. Compare this story to the one you corrected in part A of your workbook. The corrections are in **red type.**

Michiko looked at the snow falling outside her classroom window. **Michiko** did not like being cold. She always **sat** next to the heating vent, where warm air **blew** into the classroom.

Michiko's teacher said, "Everybody, I want you to write a report by next week. You can write about furnaces, dinosaurs or computers. Write a two-page paper."

Michiko **didn't** know about computers or furnaces. She **liked dinosaurs**, but she thought she might **like** to write about something else.

D. Compare this paragraph to the one you corrected in part B of your workbook. The corrections are in **red type.**

Water and milk **are** good for you to drink. **Your** body **needs** a lot of **water**, so you should **have** several glasses each day. Milk is good for your bones. **You** should also **drink** at least one glass of milk each day. But stay away from too much soda pop and sugar. Those **are** bad for you.

STOP END OF LESSON 136.

A. Compare this joke to the one you wrote.

A woman saw a boy walking down the street with carrots in his ears. She ran up to the boy and said, "Excuse me, but you have carrots in your ears."

The boy said, "What?"

The woman shouted as loud as she could, "You have carrots in your ears."

The boy said, "I'm sorry, but I can't hear you. I have carrots in my ears."

B. Use the table and the outline to write a paragraph.

	what they eat	how long they can live	body covering	how many legs
goats	plants	about 10 years	hair	four
owls	meat	about 25 years	feathers	two
lions	meat	about 25 years	hair	four
trout	meat	about 5 years	scales	none
turtles	plants and meat	about 125 years	shell	four

1. Four ways goats are different from trout
   a. Goats eat different things.
   b. Goats can live longer.
   c. Goats have a different body covering.
   d. Goats have more legs.

Independent Work

C. Compare this story to the one you corrected in part A of your workbook. The corrections are in **red type.**

After school**,** Michiko **ran** home through the snow. She opened her front door and **yelled**, "I'm home."

"**I'm** fixing dinner," her father yelled back from the kitchen. "We can eat in thirty **minutes**."

"Okay," **Michiko said**. She took off her coat**, walked** to her room and **sat** at her desk. "What am I going to write about?" she asked herself. She sat and sat, and then she **started** to feel cold.

Michiko said, "**Why** is it so cold in here? I wonder if our furnace is **working.**"

STOP END OF LESSON 137.

A. Compare this story to the one you wrote.

A crow found a nice piece of cheese. He grabbed it in his beak and flew into a tree.

A fox wanted the cheese, but she couldn't climb the tree. So she said to the crow, "I'm sure you have a beautiful voice. Could you sing me a song?"

The crow started to sing. But when he opened his beak, the cheese fell to the ground. The fox grabbed the cheese and ran away.

The story shows that you must be careful who you listen to.

B. Use the table and the outline to write a paragraph.

	how wide	length of day	hottest place
Mercury	3,031 miles	about 1,400 hours	about 800 degrees
Venus	7,520 miles	about 5,800 hours	about 890 degrees
Earth	7,926 miles	about 24 hours	about 130 degrees
Mars	4,200 miles	about 25 hours	about 80 degrees
Jupiter	88,700 miles	about 10 hours	about 40 degrees

1. Three ways Jupiter is different from Mercury
   a. Jupiter is wider.
   b. Jupiter has a shorter day.
   c. Jupiter is colder.

Independent Work

C. Compare this story to the one you corrected in part B of your workbook. The corrections are in **red type.**

    Michiko looked around her cold room. The window was closed, and everything **looked** the same as always. **Then** she **looked** at the heating vent**.** The vent **was** on the floor below the window.

    Michiko put her hand over the vent. There was no warm air coming through the vent. **"**I think I've **found** the problem,**"** she said. She **walked** down to the kitchen and asked her dad**,** "Why **isn't** any warm air coming out of my heating vent**?**"

    "I don't know," her dad answered. "**Let's** find out."

STOP END OF LESSON 138.

A. Compare this passage to what you wrote.

     The planet Mars is like Earth in some ways but different in others. Both Mars and Earth orbit the sun. Both Mars and Earth have mountains and storms. Mars even has a north pole and a south pole, just like Earth.

     But Mars is much smaller and colder than Earth. No one can live on Mars. However, because Earth has plenty of water and air, people can live here.

B. Use the table and the outline to write a paragraph.

	what they eat	how long they can live	body covering	how many legs
elephants	plants	about 60 years	hair	four
dogs	meat	about 15 years	hair	four
garter snakes	meat	about 5 years	scales	none
frogs	meat	about 5 years	skin	four
robins	plants and meat	about 10 years	feathers	two

1. Four ways elephants are different from garter snakes
   a. Elephants eat different food.
   b. Elephants can live longer.
   c. Elephants have a different body covering.
   d. Elephants have legs.

Independent Work

C. Compare this story to the one you corrected in part B of your workbook. The corrections are in **red type.**

Michiko and her dad **were** going to find out why there was no heat in her bedroom. So they **walked** down to the basement where the furnace was. Her dad pointed to big pipes that were hanging from the ceiling. He **said**, "These are called ducts. They are connected to the furnace. They **carry** warm air to every **room** in our house." Michiko **looked** at the ducts hanging from the basement ceiling**.**

"**Let's** see if the duct to your room is okay," **Michiko's** dad said. They **followed** the duct from the furnace to the corner of the basement that was under Michiko's room. After her dad looked around, he said, "I **see** the problem." The end of the duct **was** hanging down from the ceiling. It was blowing warm air into the basement and not into Michiko's room.

"I get it," said Michiko. "We need to **connect** the end of the duct to the vent in my room."

STOP END OF LESSON 139.

LESSON 140

A. Use the table and the outline to write a paragraph.

	how wide	length of day	hottest place
Mercury	3,031 miles	about 1,400 hours	about 800 degrees
Venus	7,520 miles	about 5,800 hours	about 890 degrees
Earth	7,926 miles	about 24 hours	about 130 degrees
Mars	4,200 miles	about 25 hours	about 80 degrees
Jupiter	88,700 miles	about 10 hours	about 40 degrees

1. Three comparisons of Earth and Venus
   a. Venus is almost as wide as Earth.
   b. Venus has a longer day than Earth.
   c. Venus is hotter than Earth.

B. Listen to these paragraphs.

The Kim family wants to go on a one-week vacation. Near their town is a small lake with cabins. They can drive to the lake in a few hours and then spend a whole week living in a cabin. There's not much to do at the lake except go swimming, use rowboats and sit on the beach.

The ocean is a long way from the Kims' town. They would need two days to drive there, and nobody in the family likes long car trips. At the ocean, they'd have to stay in a hotel, but there's lots to do. They can go surfing, play in the sand and ride on big fishing boats. There's also an amusement park.

Where do you think the Kims should take a vacation? Write two paragraphs to explain your answer.

- In the first paragraph, tell what you think the Kims should do. Start with the words **I think the Kims should.**
- In the second paragraph, explain why your choice is a good one. Start with the words **This is a good choice because.**

266

Independent Work

C. Compare this story to the one you corrected in part A of your workbook. The corrections are in **red type.**

Michiko's dad started to fix the duct. He **used** some tools to connect the duct to Michiko's heating vent. Suddenly **Michiko** had an idea. She could write her science report about furnaces.

Michiko **asked** her dad some questions. He **explained** how the fire in the furnace made heat. A fan inside the furnace sent the heat through the ducts to all the heating vents. Then he **showed** Michiko a short book about different kinds of heating **systems**.

Michiko read the book and **wrote** lots of notes. Then she wrote her report. **When** she was done, she told her dad, "I never used to think about furnaces. But now I can't go into a building without wondering what kind of heating system it **has.**"

STOP END OF LESSON 140.